KESI J.R. FELTON

The Morning Always Comes

reflections on being and becoming

First edition

ISBN: 979-8-9883037-0-1

This book was professionally typeset on Reedsy.
Find out more at reedsy.com

For Kés.

"Weeping may endure for a night, but joy comes in the morning."

– Psalms 30:5

Contents

Preface

Introduction: Do Nothing Without Intention

"Our stories come from our lives and from the play-wright's pen, the mind of the actor, the roles we create, the artistry of life itself and the quest for peace." — Maya Angelou

"Map your own journey, go on your own journey. Don't let others hold you back; don't hold them back. Don't judge their journey, and don't let them judge yours. All persons are free to have the experiences their souls lead them to." – Melody Beattie

(Penn)y for your thoughts – May 8, 2018, 2:10 p.m.

You would think that taking a three-day excursion to New York for an internship interview would be exciting until you find your self running late as hell on an Uber coming from Brooklyn to Penn Station.

My train was set to depart at 2:15 p.m. and where was I? Rushing down the escalators to the train track with minutes to spare after being stuck in traffic.

"You're late." Wow. Thank you, Ms. Penn Station Lady. Honestly. Thank you. I had no idea.

Feeling extremely stressed and praying I wouldn't get left behind – something I've become all too familiar with after years of trips from everywhere from Rome, Italy to Atlanta's Cumberland Mall with my grandmother, a lady with places to go – I tried my best to take the comment in stride and stay on my path, pressed towards the train to make sure I didn't get stranded over 800 miles from home.

Luckily, I made it. Barely settled in my window seat – perfect for curling up to sleep during the 10-hour overnight trip back home to Peachtree Station – I tried to calm myself down, let myself know that I made it, that I was good.

Typically, riding Amtrak solo meant that I usually wouldn't get a seat buddy until later in the trip and that I would get more room to spread out, and maybe secure a seat solely dedicated to my snack bag. This time, though, I looked up to a woman suddenly starting to put her bags in the overhead compartment and make her self comfortable in the seat next to me. Something about her seemed off. I figured that it wasn't my business and that I should just focus on relaxing and preparing for the trip ahead.

But you know how when you try to mind your business, people are still loud and clearly don't care if their business is minded...mound? Whatever. Anyways – the next thing I know this lady is on the phone with someone who seems to be yelling her ear off (might as well have been mine too). I don't remember much of the conversation's content. I do remember there being repeated calls – most of which ended with them telling her not to call back. Still trying my hardest to mind my business. There were back-and-forth calls between either a female voice (which later turned out to be her daughter) or a male voice (her husband who dropped her off at the train platform), both with similar tones and endings. I started getting a little concerned about her situation but, again, I was trying to mind my business.

When she settled in, her calls stopped, and it seemed like the train ride would be a little quieter from then on. Then, she turned to me to start a conversation – which somehow ended with her disclosing stories about her adult daughters and the aforementioned husband, whom she said she married at 19 when they had their first child. She shared other details about her life with me...she told me her name, Antonia. She talked about how she was on that train to leave an unhealthy life in New York and reclaim her life back home.

I remember her telling me at one point that she was afraid to be by her self. "You're not afraid to take the train alone?"

It was an off-putting question at first. I'd become used to traveling by myself since starting college in a city 500 miles from where I previously spent my entire life. I guess I never took a step back to really think about being a teenage girl on an overnight train 800 miles from home. I could see how someone could find that a little strange.

At that time, I was 19 years old in a weird phase of feeling overly confident like I had everything figured out in life, while simultaneously knowing deep down that I actually knew next to nothing about the world or myself.

By the end of the train ride, Antonia and I were basically besties, and by besties, I just mean I helped her take her luggage off the train when we got to her stop. Her story always stuck with me, one, because I still couldn't believe how open she was with me – a stranger – about her life, and two, because her story – being seemingly derailed off her life's path only to reclaim it and her self decades later – personified one of my worst fears.

* * *

As I sit out to write this book, I want to set a few quick house rules, Reader. First – should you decide to move forward with reading this book, I will consider us 4Lifers. Sorry, I don't make the rules.

Actually – now that I think about it, I don't think y'all need to know me like that. On a more serious note: do know that this book and its contents are very personal to me. Throughout it, I plan on sharing a wide range of stories to illustrate my experience with an identity crisis. This is not to be confused with a midlife crisis – no red sports cars or impulsive trips to the Amalfi Coast with a lover way out of my age bracket.

What I'm referring to is defined by Erik Erikson as the fifth of eight psychological crises one experiences in their life, experienced mostly by those ages 12 to 20 years old, and characterized as the "identity versus confusion of the role."

To be honest with you, Reader, to call this book an exploration of my journey through an identity crisis seems a little alarmist. It resonates more with me as the inner conflict between my ego (the outer shell formed through socialization) and my authentic self (my spirit, the essence of who I am). I often thought of this experience as a clash between the person I was raised and taught to be up until that point, and the person I have always dreamed of being. Between them stood a journey of healing, unlearning, forgiveness, releasing, and most importantly, deciding. Before employing the methods-turned-buzzword of self-actualization, I had to first decide who the fuck I actually wanted to be. Not who I have been told to be. Not what I thought I should be. I had to decide who and how I wanted to be in the world and decide to claim complete agency in that decision.

Nonetheless, I know that writing an entire book about this alleged "identity crisis" seems a little – well, very self-indulgent, so I'm going to try my best to make it more about the universal human experience, specifically for young Black women.

Here's an excerpt from a Medium article I read titled "An Identity Crisis is Vital for Change":

"Many people identify with outer aspects of their life as the basis to their identity...[some people] presume

their work, relationships, physical appearance, social and wealth status or performance are measures of their identity. Regrettably, if these aspects are removed from their life, they experience an identity crisis because they created a persona around them. **I would argue these qualities do not shape your identity but are a vehicle in which to explore your life's narrative.** *The roles you play, the features you exhibit, the things you believe in — while they matter very much in the ordinary realm of human discourse — are not what you are. When presence senses itself within you, none of these things have any substance."* [1]

Thinking back to where I started, just before my 20th birthday, I thought I had life perfectly figured out. I thought I knew what I wanted to do in life and who I wanted to be, and that it was just a matter of putting my head down and doing the work.

Most of my dreams in life were born from a desire to work myself out of complacency and mediocrity. My philosophy has long been that I didn't necessarily want to escape from my life. I did, however, recognize a level of comfort and complacency that I was afraid to passively accept, yet was resistant to fully confronting. The main obstacle in my pursuit of self-actualization was primarily a lack of clarity or certainty about what "actualization" actually meant.

I started to write this book, and it started out as a heartwarming story about the soul-searching I was doing throughout my twentieth year on the planet, about how I battled with trying to understand the person that I am today – where she came from, what led her to become who she is and how she is. But then I thought that while that was nice and could make for a truly inspiring story, I'd be letting myself off a little too easily.

This book allowed me to dig deep and confront – not necessarily my "inner demons," because me and mine don't mess with demons, amen? Rather, the subconscious parts of myself that were (and are) afraid, unsure, and even in a nihilistic way, eager to be freed of my inhibitions towards life by any means necessary. These were the parts of me I was deeply convinced would be the inevitable cause of my (ego's) demise.

After sitting with that, I realized why I was afraid to open myself fully to the world: If I did, it would eat me up, spit me out. If I share, I'll no longer be able to enjoy the things about myself, my inner world, that I held sacred. If I share, I can't control how people perceive my experiences. They would no longer be mine. I would no longer be mine. I strongly maintained a perfectionist mental model, that I couldn't put anything about myself into the world until it was 100% perfect, which resulted in intense procrastination, avoidance, and fear behind every decision I made – including the completion of this book.

As I become more entrenched in my young adulthood (read: *grown* grown), I realize identity will be something I explore in various seasons and for various reasons throughout the rest of my life. One could say there's no use in worrying about those big, existential life questions so young, but if anything this was the time for me to seriously explore what kind of person I hope to be – and all of the smaller questions that follow, that seem so far in the distance you think there's no use in wasting energy worrying about it now.

* * *

Soul-searching has almost become a buzzword in society today, defined as the "deep and anxious consideration of one's emotions and motives or of the correctness of a course of action."

If "soul-digging" were a thing, I'd call it that instead. I don't believe in soul-searching as it implies that my authentic soul is lost, somewhere out there external to me and in need of saving. I believe we come into the world fresh and new and unbruised, our souls untainted and ready to take on their next endeavor in this lifetime.

Throughout our lives, due to rearing and other methods of socialization, our souls get covered with societal expectations that ultimately decide for us what kind of person we will be in the world.

I'm a writer, so my quest was both internally and on the pages of this book – but before that, it was in the pages of journals, in my head, in my notes app, or in my therapists' offices. My goal in all of those spaces was to make sense of – in the words of my 15-year-old self – "the complex mess that is my future."

This book is a documented and more clearly curated illustration of my journey through self-exploration and steps towards identity achievement – to help me connect all the pieces of my life experiences from the past few years, and ultimately let them go.

What I've realized now as I enter the latter half of my twentieth year, especially as a young Black woman, is that we must regain agency over our lives and our self-hood. This book is a tangible declaration of that journey.

I want this book to be a manifesto of sorts for other young Black women – college-aged, those in the midst of an identity crisis or quarter-life crisis. I want to tell my story to create a space for reflection and healing for myself in a way that lets someone out there know they are not alone.

That said, here are the specific takeaways I'm hoping to leave you with via the contents of this book:

- **Claim agency over your identity and life.** – Cultivate the skill of seeing things for your self, of deciding who and how you will be. Do not allow others to tell you about your self or about the world and your place in it.
- **Once you've claimed that person, fight for them.** – Cultivate the ability to stand flat-footed and firmly rooted in the essence of who you are and who you've been called to be, especially in this world that constantly privileges the surface-level, trendy, and mediocre.
- **Question and examine everything. Including your self.** – Cultivate a practice of self-awareness,

self-examination, and self-determination, without overindulging in a never-ending stream of navel-gazing.

As I sit here writing this, wondering why I'm following through with this in the first place and second-guessing what gives me the authority to write this book, I've landed on my belief in the power of owning and sharing your story. And that I am the expert in my own lived experiences. The main reason I write is to process the very complicated ongoings of my mind, and the main reason I share my writing is for my belief in storytelling as a powerful tool for connection and change.

The underlying theme in all of these essays is identity – specifically the idea of being and becoming: Who and what I used to make sense of my self, who and what I consistently turned to through seasons of change and evolution, and who and what I clung to during challenges.

For me, the writing and re-reading of this book ground me in the following questions, that I'd like to leave with you, too: What are the truths of your life? How do you process when the truths of your life in one season change? How do you explore new possibilities and accept new truths?

Land Acknowledgments

I worked on this book over the course of four years, primarily in Acworth and Kennesaw, Georgia; Temple Hills, Maryland; Washington, D.C.; and St. Petersburg, Florida. I'd like to acknowledge the Indigenous Tribes and stewards of each of those lands:

- Cedarville Band of the Piscataway Tribe
- Anacostan (Nacotchtanks) Tribe
- Eastern Band of Cherokee Tribe
- Savannah River Band of the Uchee Tribe
- Seminole Tribe
- Tocobaga Tribe

As I learn more about efforts to better support Indigenous communities, beginning with land acknowledgment, I've thought a lot about the juxtaposition of being the descendant of stolen people, taken to stolen land for stolen labor.

Of course, this short bulleted list pales in comparison to the substantive work that we all need to commit to and participate in to rightfully repair the harm done to Indigenous peoples, and transform our collective dynamic to center their contributions and knowledge in any space – specifically in regards to our relationship with each other and the Earth.

However, I want to start wholeheartedly with this acknowledgment, and set you forth into *The Morning Always Comes* with this quote from Robin Wall Kimmerer – scientist, professor, and member of the Citizen Potawatomi Nation[2]:

"The land knows you, even when you are lost."

I hope that you're able to fully enjoy, sit with, and indulge in the experiences and perspectives shared in this book. I also hope that by the end of it, you feel a little closer to me by having read it, and more importantly that you might feel a little closer to your self by having seen a bit of your self in it. May we all be liberated by the simple act of sharing our story. Asé.

I

SELF IMAGE

"Are you sure, sweetheart, that you want to be well?... Just so's you're sure, sweetheart, and ready to be healed, cause wholeness is no trifling matter. A lot of weight when you're well." – Toni Cade Bambara, The Salt Eaters (1980)

The Realization of a Negro's Ambition

"Can't nobody fly with all that shit. Wanna fly, you got to give up the shit that weighs you down." – Toni Morrison, Song of Solomon (1977)

"Walking home, in the shoes my father bought me, I still feel I have yet to grow up." – 20 Something Manifesto

When I think of my story, where does it begin? Where did I come from? Who do I belong to? And most importantly – how did that shape my ideas about who to be and become?

I guess what feels natural is to go back to what grounds me when I need a reminder of who I am and where I come from: Storytelling and Black history (stay with me, Reader).

* * *

I recently discovered *The Realization of a Negro's Ambition* – a now-lost silent film produced in 1916 by the Lincoln Motion

Picture Company. Historical accounts of the film describe it as the first to be made by an all-Black film crew, and the first exploration of the Black middle-class experience on screen.

Here's the plot, according to The Department of Afro-American Research, Arts, and Culture's Archive:

> "James Burton, a young Negro graduate from Tuskegee, as a civil engineer finds no satisfaction working on his father's farm and heads west. Unable to find a job because of his color, he is despondent. He chances upon a runaway two-horse rig and risks his life to stop it. Unknowingly, he saved the daughter of an oil company owner. Out of gratitude, he's given a job as head of oil expeditions. He convinces the owner to let him drill on his father's farm and surrounding farms. After a round of trickery and romance, he strikes oil and is soon wealthy. He buys a home and gets married. The last scene shows James in later years, with ambition realized: home and family, a nice country to live and nice people to live by and enjoy it with him."[3]

Interestingly, Lincoln Motion Picture Company was originally founded in Omaha, Nebraska; where roughly 30 years after the debut of *The Realization of a Negro's Ambition*, my grandfather's family made their way to Omaha from Yazoo, Mississippi, for a better life and opportunities, specifically in the city's meat-packing factories.

4

* * *

Fast-forward another two generations: Hi, I'm Kési – pronounced "Casey," not "Kessie". My full name is Kési Joyce Roxanne Felton. Joyce after my Granny, Joyce, and Roxanne after my great-aunt Roxann.

I was born in Atlanta, Georgia, and raised in a relatively small town called Acworth, where I grew up with my mom, dad, and little brother. Home life was pretty chill, nothing problematic or Capital 'T' Traumatic. Got to do a decent amount of traveling with my grandparents and cousins which I always enjoyed.

I come from a family of Black folks who are Southern (and Midwestern – go Cornhuskers!), God-fearing, educated (overwhelmingly by Historically Black Colleges and Universities), and all pretty well-accomplished and involved in their communities – the communities in question mainly being Metro Atlanta, Georgia; St.Petersburg, Florida; Omaha, Nebraska; and Chicago, Illinois.

I was always taught – well, side note: my mom used to tell me about using "always" and "never" which I alwa- often think about...so – I was brought up to value my education, world travel, family, being a kind person...all the traits of a Good Samaritan. I guess I was considered one of the "gifted kids" in school – I loved learning but hated all the rules and authority. Most people know and remember me to be shy and quiet. Some would say a rule-follower, although I'd disagree – I'm more of a do-what-I-want-but-still-play-it-safe kinda girl.

I've loved to write since I was young (hence this book), so when it came time for me to pick a major for college I was pretty set on studying journalism at Howard University – which I might add is in the same school my mom graduated from in '91, and my dad from its law school in '93.

My first two years of college were great – moved to D.C., and gained a level of independence that really showed me how sheltered I was growing up back home, I regularly saw celebrities on campus in between classes, on the Yard, or during Homecoming (sometimes a combination of the three at Yardfest), I (allegedly) overslept for my School of C(ommunications) 8 a.m.'s more times than I can count but not too many times to fail the class, I [redacted], and [redacted] – and I can't forget that one weekend where [redacted]. That was wild. And just so my parents don't think their money was wasted, I did learn a good bit about AP Style, so yeah. Those first two years were truly a great time.

Overall, I was loving my experience at Howard and learning so much about the world and what I wanted to achieve in it. It was so life-affirming to be around so many like-minded Black folks who looked like me and were equally as motivated to be successful and change the world.

* * *

Growing up, I didn't necessarily have to worry about the responsibility of life, so I often stressed about the day I'd have to assume that responsibility for myself. Given the capitalistic society we live in, much of that anxiety I easily attributed to money and achievement.

I often thought of life's journey like you're floating down a river: I'd simply surrender to the current and (hopefully) end up in the right place. Somewhere safe and comfortable.

Being sheltered in life is something I don't necessarily take for granted, but I can say it became a crutch that gave me permission to remain complacent. I try to understand what it took for my parents, grandparents, and even great-grandparents to be able to build the lives they have had and to offer me the life and opportunities I've had. But I also took comfort in knowing that if I put in no extra work, I'd be "okay."

What I internalized about money and what it was for, the purpose it was supposed to serve in one's life – was that it was more a tool to manufacture and present a certain image for others, to create a level of comfort for oneself in a singular, present moment.

Money's inextricable connection to time and energy, and the outcomes you're able to produce with them, was something I also struggled with as I tried to find my place in our society that thrives on "hustle culture." I thought the inevitable hardships or uncertainties I would face in life – and the fervent anxiety I felt about them when it related to materiality[4] was something one could work through with #PositiveVibes and – in my own, 15-year-old words – "work harder" and "do better."

My meaning of success was driven by a directive to avoid discomfort through accumulating money and praise, and understandably so, but there was a part of me that would've rather believed that, for me, success would mean something deeper than that. BJ the Chicago Kid said it best (or rather, sang it best, with beautifully layered harmonies): "'Cause when I die, you know I can't take none of this with me no-no-no-no."[5]

I think that way of relating to money taught me to be worry-free when I "had it" and unable to demonstrate resilience when the opposite was true. I believe those standards also stemmed from the assumption that success – and the journey towards it – is always supposed to look and feel good. I've since learned that sometimes success may look and feel like a season of struggle, but you ultimately end up growing on a much deeper level than you otherwise would have, which is exactly what happened after that train ride from New York.

* * *

I was already becoming disillusioned by the seemingly never-ending cycle of Internship SZN somehow being every season – the constant barrage of opportunities that I could never quite tell if I wasn't right for it, or if it wasn't right for me. Being ghosted by a particular online magazine after traveling to a whole 'nother state for the interview may or may not have solidified that feeling (it's fine, I'm fine). I figured it (read: receiving the employer's equivalent of a "u up?" text asking if I still wanted to work there) might've been a sign for me to stop worrying about it so much and trust myself more, instead of perpetually waiting on the edge of my seat for external validation.

But that wasn't really the point. The point was: the mere idea of that experience – not getting a summer internship – was scary because it triggered my overwhelm with the fact that there was so much about what I wanted to do with my life that I still needed to learn, and it felt like not getting those opportunities was holding me back from achieving that. There was a set of goals I had at that point in my life and one perceived path that I had to take to achieve that set of goals. Deep down I believed experience within an already established institution was the only kind of valid experience. The idea of creating or cultivating my own opportunities wasn't necessarily scary, but I was more concerned with how my path to success would be perceived and if it...if I...would be taken seriously.

I used to think that my ego – the character that I subconsciously (and at times, consciously) perform for the world – was a version of myself who had these larger-than-life dreams and that my authentic self was more grounded and realistic with what she would accomplish in the world. I realize now that it is actually the opposite.

My authentic self, more specifically the version of myself connected to and led by my inner child, is a dreamer through and through. She sees no limits to her capabilities in this life. Everything she envisions, she believes is well within her right to actualize.

As I've gotten older, I began to internalize the dream-killer that is "being realistic" because of fear. I've prioritized playing it safe above showing up authentically and pursuing my deepest desires for my life. Even more so, I internalized a very real fear of – for a lack of better words – fucking my life up. In a more eloquent and family-friendly way: the fear of failing to acquire material security, survive, and simply do life well.

I once read an article in *The Atlantic* about how Black middle-class American children have a higher likelihood of falling into poverty than their white counterparts. If I wasn't unsure of my life's path already, that article for sure confirmed my deepest fears about the future, reminding me that my slightly above-average intellect and suburban upbringing seemed to check the boxes on paper, but it did not ensure my material security in the future.[6]

Of course, I should want to make sure I can eat, have a roof over my head, and be able to enjoy nice things and be comfortable in life, but I didn't want that to be the end all be all. I wanted to be able to go to sleep every night knowing I was on the right path to become the best version of myself I could be while positively impacting my community and exploring all life has to offer.

I often have Colossians 3:2 in the back of my mind, "Set your minds on things that are above, not on things that are on Earth." I thought I knew that when your goals don't go beyond the material world, they lay on a faulty foundation. You could lose your job, house, car, or any other belongings in an instant, but you could never lose your purpose.

I was becoming more and more aware that this world and its social structure make it extremely hard for people to meet their material needs, especially marginalized people. Capitalist systems, in particular, render millions of people to a lifetime of surviving and barely keeping their heads above water. No matter how much I tried to avoid understanding that reality, I began to see how it catalyzed my fears about my belief in my ability to meet my own material needs as an adult.

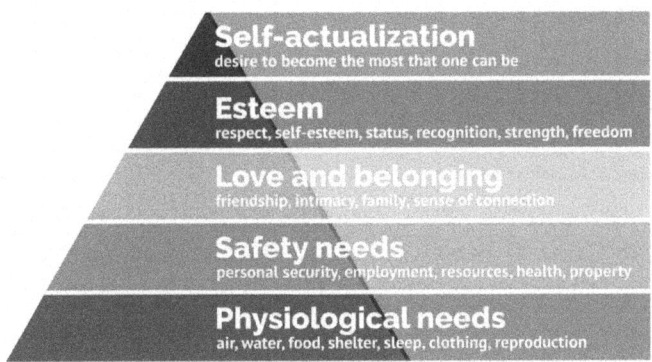

Maslow's Hierarchy of Needs (Source: Simply Psychology)[7]

This concept is most notably illustrated by Maslow's Hierarchy of Needs. It isn't meant to be a strict, prescriptive guide on the steps to take to win at life, rather an invitation to think about how human beings understand and meet our most basic needs. People's esteem, capacity to connect to others, or their ability to self-actualize may and often is rooted in their ability to meet their most basic material needs. So when those seemingly basic things are made difficult to obtain consistently, people can very well explore bits and pieces of the other levels on the pyramid, but that doesn't absolve their right to have those most basic material needs fully met.

* * *

This fear subconsciously put me in a prolonged state of dependency so that I wouldn't have to be fully on my own in the deep end and, more importantly, totally culpable if I failed. For a period of time, it felt like that was working, that I was getting by on some path forward. I could keep going down the path of least resistance – the one where I checked the boxes and ended up at the end of the river and left this life feeling...okay...with it. As I gained more independence and access to the world through my college experiences, the conversations changed from just getting in the door to simply gain experience, to learning how to navigate pay negotiations so I could stop accepting unpaid internships, fielding questions about what my plan was for post-grad – because it was becoming less of a far-off idea and more of a reality that I had to start thinking about. All of this triggered my underlying fears and created an internal resistance to those opportunities altogether.

There was a part of me that feared having a lot of money and subsequently, responsibility. Like...adult amounts of it? Is that a thing that I should be allowed to have and experience? Me? The girl who has been told periodically throughout life that she can't do anything right? Are you sure?

The idea of having to be responsible for "Big Things" terrified me. I was afraid because I didn't trust myself to successfully maintain, grow, or recover "Big Things" if I lost them or fucked them up. I was afraid that if I claimed full responsibility for my life and failed, there would be no coming back from that. Forget the idea of one day becoming someone's partner, mother, or having any other influence in someone else's life. The idea of being responsible for others in any meaningful way made me want to disappear.

And so, pretty much my whole life, I did just that. I made it so that the only thing I ever had to worry about was me, myself, and I. When I would inevitably fuck up, the only person who had to feel the ramifications of that failure was me. A lot of times, the only person who had to know that failure even took place, was me.

* * *

The following semester after that train ride from New York, it turned out that I wasn't sure if I'd be able to continue my matriculation at school. As we just discussed, you might conclude that the mere idea of having to leave shook up my entire sense of how I thought this stage of my life would be unfolding. It sent me into an anxious overdrive to find any way to stay enrolled (read: to try to save face and salvage what was left of my grip on my comfort zone – proudly sponsored by the privilege of simply never having gone through some shit).

Even deeper than that, it chipped the first crack in my ego,

13

the ego that depended on the illusion of material success and achievement – and particularly my ability to consistently exhibit progress thereto – to maintain its hold on my identity and self-worth.

Me? A Hero?

"[The Hero fears] letting go of their defenses and showing themselves as they truly are. They are afraid, it seems, that if they were to allow themselves to be trusting, something terrible would happen to them." – *Pierre-E. Lacocque,* Fear of Engulfment and the Problem of Identity (1984)

"Deal with your self as an individual worthy of respect and make everyone else deal with you the same way." – *Nikki Giovanni*

By the end of my sophomore year, I was starting to get involved in campus life and felt like I was making strides toward getting my feet wet in all things writing, journalism, content creation – things that I started to gain a passion for but never had the space to dedicate a lot of time to in high school.

These extracurriculars were a great way for me to begin to find my self, explore my interests, and discover who I was as a storyteller and leader. And although I loved them, my personal projects and extracurriculars became increasingly demanding over time, to say the least: Between my sophomore and junior years I wound up with multiple visits to urgent care due to stress-related inflammation and a super gnarly eczema rash...also severely worsened by stress.

I later came to realize (through therapy and lots of self-reflection) that much of that stress – and specifically, as a result of my inability to say "no" (or, really, I'd like to reframe it as the inability to stop saying "yes") – was rooted in a need to perpetually overcompensate and justify my existence through my accomplishments and the illusion of progress towards them.

At the start of my sophomore year of high school: I created a DIY-decorated journal – complete with printed and glued-on cutouts of Howard's blue and red logo, the brochure-approved photo of Founder's Library on The Yard, a picture of Venus Williams from when I saw her play in the first round of the 2011 U.S. Open, some of my favorite bible verses and motivational quotes (including one from a Panda Express fortune cookie fortune) – all to get me motivated for the upcoming school year.

"In case I ever feel like quitting, I can come back to this and regain the ambition I have now...To be honest, I'm just tired of not being successful 100% of the time. Well, actually, 100% seems unrealistic so 90-95% of the time...[T]his journal isn't to pour my heart onto each page or ramble about irrelevant things going on in my life, this is to document my journey to a successful year in high school and in life in general."

It's safe to say my standards for my own success in life at 15 years old were…a lot. The clear declaration of that journal not being a place to "pour my heart out or ramble about irrelevant things" was (and is) super on brand. Looking back, I believe those standards came from internalizing the voices of people around me who expected a lot from me, without really helping me understand the inner workings of what a successful life actually meant, what it could look and feel like, and how I could cultivate one for my self.

I came to the realization that nobody is depending on me to be successful. I see my peers who have to work their way through school, who are first-generation college students and graduates, who are working class and trying to simply pay their bills and get by in life. They have people that are depending on them to be successful. Plenty of people in my family who have degrees (plural) are successful and have made lives and careers for themselves. Nobody needs me to make it.

Am I doing good? Am I on the right track? Or am I drifting along passively for the Earth to inevitably crumble beneath and around me?

I've witnessed and internalized what my parents and grand-parents sacrificed or did for me to be here. My grandfathers left their homes for better opportunities, and my grandmoth-ers went with them, their families, and their communities down in the process.

One thing I can definitely give my parents credit for is that I know what peace and stability feel like in my body and my home.

Your parents and grandparents have done their work, and your ancestors have lived their lives. What will I be able to say about my own journey?

* * *

> *"Flying was a new freedom and made Icarus feel invincible, even if his wings were mere wax and feathers. Even if it was for a moment before the Sun's heat melted his wings, Icarus felt like he could actually be something great." – The Myth of Icarus: Chasing the Sun*

I think that my Achilles Heel is pervasive self-doubt. Some might call that Imposter Syndrome, which tracks. I feel a pervasive and constant pressure to prove my self, to defy my inner critic saying that I'm not good enough or I'm too small or weak to be anything great.

I am a firm believer in everyone's positive potential – including my own. But what about negative potential?

I can't trust the highs, because if you get too high, the harder the fall. The lows anchor you – either in a *weigh-you-down, Toni Morrison, Erykah Badu "Bag Lady"* kind of way, or in a predictable, safe, comfortable, and familiar way. Staying close to the ground feels safe, predictable…familiar.

But then, the question becomes, "Who am I pretending to be? And for what gain? To what end?" Maybe it's a version of my self that I think I should be. The version of my self that I think would be worthy of success, love, peace. Happiness.

That still doesn't answer the question: *Who* is that person? My gut reaction is telling me that all of the things I am not are what I need to change. All of the things I can't change are the things I need to compensate for by working harder and being better than my shortcomings.

What do I need to do in order to be and become who I'm meant to be and become?

Maybe it's a lack of belief in my self? Maybe it's doubt about whether I truly believe there is room for all of me – my (honest and authentic) wants, needs, emotions, and thoughts.

Notes – undated

My thoughts ideas and questions about who I am and what I want to be and do with my life

- *"Withholding info about that which they are uncertain"*
- *Fear of not knowing*

Nobody really engaged with your ideas and feelings; what you thought and felt about the world and your self and your life

- *What do you think about X?*
- *Why do you think that is? Why do you think that is the way*

that is? Where did that thought originate from?
- *How do you feel about that?*
- *Where do you think that feeling originated from?*

There is a deep discomfort in not knowing. Not knowing who I am. Who I truly want to be for my self. How to bridge the gap between the two. The only tool I knew to use was to think and research and write my way closer to an answer.

So, in the spirit of giving voice to my inner world and, more specifically, my navel-gazing: Where do those thoughts and beliefs come from?

If we start with childhood, that time, for me at least, was about internalizing the constant, incessant external gaze by way of behavioral correction from adults.

In terms of the "who" and "how" to be, I was supposed to be good, stay in the lines, doing what I should or ought to be doing.

What I learned subconsciously, through the correction and constant awareness of the external gaze was that being seen and taking up space was not a safe or comfortable place for me to just be. If you get called out, you're being disruptive, doing the wrong thing, or making a mistake.

So, I learned early that if I stay small, out of the way, and to my self, I'll be safe. I won't cause any problems for anyone or my self.

Tumblr Post – Age 13

I'm sitting here trying as hard as possible to do this paper when I was given a week to do it, and most likely won't complete it...I know it's my fault and I should fail and know I will...I don't work nearly as hard as my classmates, who are all probably working their asses off trying to perfect their speeches right now. My teacher even told me that I should reconsider doing magnet and I completely agreed with him. I didn't want to sign up for magnet and really wish my parents didn't make me. And my mom told me that I obviously should be in magnet because I was accepted, but that only means that I can pass a standardized test and write an okay essay. My problem with school is that I just don't take it seriously enough and I have horrible time management skills.

Although I'm excited to be leaving middle school, I'm really scared to go to high school, because I'm afraid I'm going to fail. I have the idea that I'm not going to be as smart as the other kids and I'm going to fall behind and not be able to catch up. It's scary thinking about balancing magnet, marching band, and tennis. I don't want to have to give anything up but I probably will. I'm hoping I can get it together and balance everything and not have to give anything up because these are all things I've wanted to do for a really long time.

And there's another thing, the one thing that pisses me off the most in this whole situation is myself. I have every power to do my homework, not procrastinate, and make better grades, but I just don't and I have no idea why. I sit there and get distracted KNOWING that I had this important assignment to do and think

"Oh well I can do it later" then have the nerve to want to complain about it. That's the one thing I don't like about this situation and it's the main thing I don't like about myself as a person. I have a majority of the power to get to where I want to be in life, yet I sit around thinking that God's gonna do all the work. That's not true at all, from my perspective, God has the plan, I just have to put it into action.

* * *

In that, I looked for things – people, experiences, maybe a sign, or an omen (word to *The Alchemist*[8]) – to affirm me, or that resonated with me to let me know that *I* was possible.

To assuage my self-doubt and clear my emotional residue from not feeling seen and supported in reaching someone else's vision of success, versus seeking support for my own definition and vision.

Society teaches us to navigate fear and uncertainty – things we don't yet understand or know – with control and domination. Either externally or internally by eroding our human responses and emotions and shaming our selves for having and experiencing fear, or for simply not knowing.

I felt the pressure and expectation, but I don't feel like anyone actually held space to ask me what I wanted, or tried to facilitate the journey of discovering what I wanted.

I felt as though people and the institutions they represented were not really invested in the impact of those expectations on me as a human being, just about how it stroked their ego and reflected back onto them and the success of their journeys and roles.

Who actually has a vested interest in who you actually become?

During major transitions or periods of perceived uncertainty, I go inward and do what is always been true about me as a human; to adapt to whatever my new normal is becoming, and establish internal certainty, some sense or source of truth, and inner knowing

I see it mainly as a means of self-preservation. A way to somehow prevent the progression of the loss as much as possible. It helps to soothe the fear I am losing time and opportunities to live the life of my dreams, by rooting my self deeply in the familiar.

I have always felt more moved to stay in the periphery of spaces I belonged in that gave the illusion of progress towards success. I liked the communal experience of having shared goals and vision for growth and elevation. College was the space where I started to discover that – where I could think and imagine and dream and create whatever I wanted in my little inner world, and share what I wanted to be collectively experienced (after the fact, though).

During this time, I responded by becoming even more closed off, more to my self, more self-reliant; and subsequently internalizing much more stress and anxiety in trying to process and make sense of where I was at by my self.

I was always afraid that I'd open my self up to "Well what did you do or not do? Have you tried ___?" (i.e. the obvious things) as opposed to a kind, empathetic, and compassionate "What have you tried? What do you need? How can we support you?"

When people give you advice or suggestions for your life, they often do so by ignoring the current state of emotions or thoughts you may currently be in.

How much more validating and compassionate might it be if we lightly touched the current thoughts and feelings, acknowledged their existence as it currently is – and simultaneously acknowledged each other's, or our own, internal realities – and then lightly nudged one another towards a possible way of seeing, doing, or being that might end up being more healthy, fulfilling, beneficial, for that person (or our selves).

Giving my self the room to say, "I see why you feel safer up here, why you tend to hold on to this old way of being. It held you and got you to where you are today. However, what possibilities might you be ignoring or foregoing altogether, that are on the other side of you releasing this old way of being?"

That version acknowledges the deeper feeling or root cause of what the person may be struggling with or holding on to, without affirming a victim mentality or callously pushing them towards a new thing without taking the time to be empathetic to the reason they held onto the old thing.

What my apprehension to be open has been all along, was the fear of not knowing. Of not knowing the answer in class, to a more existential not knowing my self and who I thought I should be and become. I don't know what the difference was, but the first step to my healing was enlisting the same tools I had always used in private, but this time to turn that journey to self-understanding outwards.

Even more deeply, I was afraid of opening the proverbial can of worms: Confirming that I did actually fly too close to the Sun, that I am a burden, that I am over-complicated, and that I overcomplicate things for others with the space I take up.

That I assumed expectations when there weren't any, that I assigned my self the task of overthinking about how to measure up to everyone's expectations, if it was even possible at all.

Deep down, I think I'm secretly angry about the fact that no one has told me what to do or who to be. That I have to create her from scratch. That I have no pre-existing blueprint to rebel against. No prescribed destiny to dispute. Like everyone else on this rock we call Earth, I have no manual or guide to help me figure out the journey. That I feel overwhelmed by the complexity of life and the fact that it's so big with so many different possibilities and ways to experience it. That I will inevitably have to reckon with the fact that I can't live all of those experiences at once (or maybe at all).

I feel constant conflict and friction and tension between emotional isolation and a desperate need for agency, and a deep desire for connection and belonging to something bigger than me.

Maybe, I can choose who I get to be and live as large or small a life as I please. That I can choose to utilize the wealth of information this world has to offer to inform my decisions and set the foundation for a life that exudes love, impact, and legacy. That I can simply choose to show up in the fullness of who God has called me to be in every phase of my life, and see where it leads me.

That I actually don't need anyone's permission to do it.

With that, I still grapple with what I *should* want. I know that I want what it wants me back. I want what God has for me. I want what the Universe will make space for me to experience with ease.

When I would see other people experience and achieve the things I wanted, it triggered me. I tried to reframe it as an invitation to check back in with my self about my progress with my ego. "Yes, you did want that at one point in time. You might very well still want that. If it's meant to be, it'll come to you with ease and in Divine timing."

So I guess it is up to me to explore and decide what success – for me, by my own standards and of my own volition – looks and feels like, and whether I want it in the way I thought I was supposed to want it, let alone at all.

I can't say that I have the utmost conviction about the journey I'm actually meant to be on.

All I know is that I'm here – healthy and with breath in my lungs. That, for right now, I can sit in the present moment with openness and curiosity about who I am and why I'm here. That who and how I am at this moment doesn't have to be all there is.

But that part will figure itself out in due time.

There's no resistance here, to be honest. It's a beautiful place to be. but there are moments where again, I question if there's more work to do, things to learn, things to unlearn. but there are also moments where I accept the invitation to just allow whatever is to just be. To just accept what the Universe has offered in the present moment without unnecessary resistance because that doesn't mean that there isn't still growth to be had, things to experience and accomplish, or lessons to learn. It just means you moved out of conflict with your self and with the Universe and with God, and into alignment and harmony with what already is and will be.

* * *

For now, I guess it's up to me to be incredibly present – to try to not focus on the future so much that I miss opportunities to show up and act in the present moment and to be so held down by the past that I don't allow my self to fully explore and experience the breadth of my potential.

Who am I supposed to be? Does it truly matter at the end of the day? Who has a vested interest in my success and in my life to turn out how it's meant to turn out?

I don't know that there's any one spectacular outcome or person that I'm supposed to or aspiring to become. I don't even know if the point is to forget about all the achieving and becoming and solely focus on being. There's something to be explored about focusing my time and energy and focus on leaning into the tension and balance between the two.

There are moments when you focus so much on being that life feels stagnant.

Other times, you focus too much on becoming that you run the risk of missing the little moments life has to offer. Moving too much that you forget what it feels like to be still. God forbid you build a life that doesn't allow you to ever be still.

I believe that we all have to sit with the chasms between who we aspire to be in the future, who we believe our selves to be in the present moment, and the truth of who we are.

In that space – specifically between the latter two – can exist a lot of shame. It can cause us to look for approval and unhealthy validation, as opposed to healthy validation as stepping stones to love and acceptance of our selves and others. It can lead us to create habits and mindsets that give us permission to beat our selves up to get from point A to point B – it can include unhealthy comparison, the emboldening of a harsh inner critic, and even self-hatred or contempt.

We fear and avoid the truth because we may inadvertently validate what critics have said or say about us, as well as the things about our selves that we think may prove that we are unlovable or not worthy of the things that we want.

I don't want to act like I have no shortcomings at all, or like my shortcomings can't or don't have real implications and consequences for my self and others. However, I am no longer accepting that as the sole truth that I choose to put at the forefront of my self-concept and story.

While there is a version of my self who is unsure, full of self-doubt, and who second-guesses her self constantly; there is also a version of my self who is convicted and clear about who she is and what she wants out of life.

I believe that what I need(ed) is a sufficient acknowledgment of my fear, anxiety, worry, and doubt. Reassurance that it is normal and okay to be unsure or admit what you don't yet know or are not yet able to embody.

In the wise words of The Cheetah Girls, "I don't wanna be like Cinderella/Sitting in a dark, cold, dusty cellar/Waiting for somebody to come and set me free."[9]

Freedom once meant achieving the goals that society said you should achieve in order to find success and happiness.

Freedom once felt like not having to be actively engaged in my own life to achieve that – to just be and accept the course you were already on.

Journeying towards your best self while hoping something that they are or have might save you, keeps you uselessly hopeful. And most importantly, I believe it keeps you dependent on systems that are counting on you believing that endless labor on the hamster wheel of material success is true liberation.

What does success even mean – period, let alone to me personally?

They say that the reward for good work is more work. And, honestly, that terrified me. With that, my idea of success contorted into a deep desire for freedom. Freedom from. Freedom to.

What role does feeling seen or heard – either by the world around us leading to us being able to see or hear our own authentic selves or not – play in our ability to take control of our lives and make the transition to adulthood? To decide who and how we want to be in the world? How do I imagine my self at my fullest potential? How do I imagine the world at its fullest potential? How do I imagine my self influencing and being influenced in the world? Of course, I can't control all of the circumstances that will shape me, but the exercise forces you to think about where your dreams and aspirations start and stop, where they come from, and to whom they belong.

It's about not accepting everything at face value, but deeply examining your self to uncover the person you're actually meant to be in the world and work to align your self with her. It's about being clear about the parts of your life you do have control over and exerting agency over your part while allowing your self to influence and be influenced.

Liberation: Being able to live life on your own terms (self-determination), even when your own mental blockages are what is holding you back. Liberation is knowing clearly what I can and can't control in life, and making decisions from that place. I can't change how other people perceive me, and that is not my battle to fight. But what I can control is showing up fully as my authentic self. Liberation is "no fear" in the words of Nina Simone. A lot of my dreams about who and how I wanted to be in the world were out of fear.

So of course my concept of freedom feels different now. It's not different in a bad way, it's just the realization that my previous goal – of simply following the expectations set before you – is no longer serving you – and I am being invited to find a new North Star.

So, what do freedom and liberation mean to me? Who or what would I be liberating my self from?

- Freedom from my desire to avoid responsibility and power over others to choose personal agency and power over my self
- Freedom from the idea of double consciousness, constantly viewing my self from other people's perspective instead of getting to know my self and acting in favor of my own wants and needs
- Freedom from other people's expectations or limited definitions of who I am and who I can become, particularly

THE MORNING ALWAYS COMES

based on race and gender, without getting to know my own desires and motivations
- Freedom from needing validation or permission to become the person I know I am and am meant to become
- Freedom from internal biases and prejudices that prevent me from being an effective member of the movement toward true collective Black liberation, starting with my self
- Freedom from my own self-doubt to just be who I am and who I've always been

More affirmatively, what are you seeking freedom *to*? What is the destination point? How will you know you've made it there?

- Freedom to create a Universe from my inner world and invite others to share that with me – in my relationships, through my writing, etc.
- Freedom to decide and act on what I want without considering the myriad ways it might impact others
- Freedom to see and experience parts of my self and my life and the world for my self
- Freedom to choose who and how to be, irrespective of the blueprint that you have been given and the responsibility of carrying that on in its original form
- Freedom to decide the pace, speed, direction, and intention with which I move toward my goal(s)
- Freedom to be able to acknowledge that right now I just have me – and to let that be good enough.

And if nobody cares or has a vested interest in my journey

toward that, do I still care?

* * *

The way I thought of and processed my own experience, specifically in the writing of this book, was through the Hero's Journey. When I think of the Hero's Journey I think of Odyssey, Hercules (the Disney version, of course), or any of his Greek counterparts. I think of Harry Potter. Honestly, I could think of a few more popular stories of white boys' Hero's Journeys, but that's not the point – or maybe it is…I definitely can't say I've seen or heard the story of a Black girl or woman going through their own Hero's Journey – notably theorized by Professor Joseph Campbell – but we'll come back to that.

Here's how Campbell conceptualized the infamous Hero's Journey:

> *"A hero ventures forth from the world of common day into a region of supernatural wonder: fabulous forces are there encountered and a decisive victory is won: the hero comes back from this mysterious adventure with the power to bestow boons on his fellow man."*[10]

If you're not sure what a "boon" is, you're not alone, but anywho…researcher and psychologist Pierre-E. Lacocque explores the Hero's Journey as symbolism for the personal journey that us everyday folk go on to dive deeper into self-exploration and to conquer our demons. The inner kind, not the three-headed dragon kind, and certainly not the d*vilish kind.

In *"Fear of Engulfment and the Problem of Identity (1984)*[11]*,"* Lacocque describes Carl E. Jung's interpretation of the Hero's Journey as a symbol for the search for meaning:

> *"The 'treasure hard to find,' as he calls it, is in fact the knowledge of and mastery over the unconscious processes and desires." (pg. 220)*

I would never flatter my self enough to say that my experience this chapter of my life elicited my own mini Hero's Journey, per se. But it did, however, take me down a journey of intense self-reflection and questioning of everything I thought I was and wanted in life. "It" being the complete disruption of what I thought was leading up to a textbook, check-all-the-boxes, straightforward life well-lived. It absolutely forced me to question where I sought meaning, a purpose, and my foundational sense of self. But, to be thorough, and for my own humility, let's take a deeper look at Jung's definition:

> *"[H]eroism for Jung has two basic components attached to it. First, it means risking being alone with oneself... It means relinquishing the great temptation to have someone fully caring for or protecting us. A hero is one who is not afraid of the messages of the unconscious and one who allows them to shape consciousness. But ultimately, it means longing for a better, more peaceful*

world to live in, both for oneself and for humankind as a whole. Heroes aim toward such a goal by assuming the roles of models and teachers. Through these, they point the way to how to live life while in relationship with the divine." (222)

That's what I so desperately needed: to reach the point of a more peaceful inner life and to fully take the reins on my journey toward becoming my highest, most aligned self.

I later learned that the Hero's Journey concept, for all intents and purposes (read: for the intents and purposes of my narrative), aligns with Erik Erikson's Identity Development Theory, specifically the "identity crisis." It's described as "a period of uncertainty and confusion in which a person's sense of identity becomes insecure, typically due to a change in their expected aims or role in society."

The rest of the Identity Development Theory idea gets at our journey in life to make sense of who we are in the world through the exploration of options of who we want to become, the discovery of who that person might be (or a composite of bits and pieces that get close to them), and a commitment those one or several characteristics and, ultimately, our true identity. Needless to say, Erikson called this "Identity Achievement."

Reaching identity achievement highlights an important part of what Lacocque discussed in their research, which I've eloquently summed up here: Unless life gives you no choice, why the fuck would anyone do that of their own volition? But here's the fancy, academic version:

> *"What is there to be gained by risking the plunge into one's depths? What do heroes find in the underworld or at bottoms of oceans? Eliade responds, 'One goes down into the belly of a giant or monster in order to learn science or wisdom.' The hero is now a person who knows. He has learned the mysteries surrounding life and is one who was given revelations that are metaphysical in nature. To face one's demons and to succeed in taming them implies that one no longer fears the disintegration of the self." (222)*

I don't know about "disintegration," but I certainly feared the idea of having to live a life that differed from the trajectory I believed I was on.

I forget at what point the external critics became my internal voice, but she constantly made me feel that if I learn more and know more then I can avoid failure altogether. But if I have and know everything I need and still fail, then what? Is it worth it if I become everything I'm "supposed to" become, at the expense of my peace, happiness, relationships, and connections with my self and others?

Is it about the outcome or the process? History doesn't favor losers, even when the person who lost can accept that they failed.

> *"As gruesome and frightening as the heroes' ordeals might be, they nonetheless fascinate. They appeal to our imagination because they offer a possible answer to the perennial unfinished business we have with our selves: how to separate from the safe and the known and find ways to confront life on firm ground, alone, yet unafraid."* (225)

I don't think I feel entitled to a happy ending, but I genuinely have no other frame of reference to make sense of who and how I should be in the world. But, as I said before, I'm a writer – and if we're keeping up with the Hero's Journey analogy – I'm guessing that I'm now in the face of that plunge into the unknown, yet unable to skip ahead to the end of the story where I can rest knowing that I've won the "battle."

And so this, Dear Reader, is my Hero's Journey – where I am both the hero and the villain. The person in need of saving, and the only person worthy enough to endure the quest. And so my journey begins.

When God Speaks Through Your Uber Driver

"Freeing your self was one thing, claiming ownership of that freed self was another." – Toni Morrison, Beloved (*1987*)

"Who taught you to hate the texture of your hair? Who taught you to hate the color of your skin?...Who taught you to hate the shape of your nose and the shape of your lips? Who taught you to hate your self from the top of your head to the soles of your feet? Who taught you to hate your own kind? Who taught you to hate the race that you belong to so much so that you don't want to be around each other? [Y]ou should ask your self who taught you to hate being what God made you." – Malcolm X, Who Taught You to Hate your self? (*1962*)

Are you sure you want to be well?

M y subconscious response during the first part of my gap year was to take on as few responsibilities as possible outside of internships. To essentially become a hermit and work on my own personal projects (for which there are no real consequences if I failed or didn't follow through).

As I write, the quote "to whom much is given, much is required" comes to mind. But what if you don't want it? The thing you've been given: your purpose.

I was still in D.C., so I remained connected to campus while working in the city. I don't really remember much from the first couple of months around that time anymore. I was creating a little, putting on community events for my media organization Better to Speak, and co-hosting a podcast through a campus-owned and student-led radio station. So on the surface (and by on the surface I mean based on my archived Instagram posts), things seemed like they were fine.

I remember I started to take production classes at DCTV, a local public broadcasting station. It was an attempt to keep learning and growing despite not being at Howard. It was a great opportunity to get exposed to other things in the D.C. community outside of the Howard bubble, and it taught me about TV and video production, specifically to tell the stories of those who don't always have a platform to do so.

I remember that being a period of time where I started going to church again fairly regularly. I had gotten involved with the audio production team and was attending events outside of Sunday service every now and again.

I remember reading (and actually finishing!) books during my commutes to and from work. I made a habit of taking selfies at the bus stop and Metro (somehow this was a great skin era for me) and by the end of my fellowship, I went home with an internship secured at the ACLU of Georgia. The goal was to learn about my home state's political scene and start building community and professional relationships.

I also remember going through a period of binge eating – which I don't think I've ever shared with anyone besides my therapist at the time. I guess triggered by a combination of the lack of control over my situation with school, and the fact that I was spending my entire paycheck on rent. So that anxiety about not being able to meet some of my material needs? Yeah, very much triggered.

But aside from that, it seemed like I was still moseying along my path, making progress toward my goals given the uncertainty of my circumstance.

I remember being in my final session with my first therapist, I let her know about all the things I was doing to keep my self busy and working towards my goals despite not being in school.

I remember her looking at me for a moment before responding, "I'm hearing you talk, and you don't seem truly motivated or happy."

Why would she say that? I was mitigating this problem by finding another avenue to keep moving forward. I was moving forward – and that was good, right?

Maybe I was simply saying yes to things to have something to look forward to. Something to keep me anchored and oriented toward the future…*a* future. Something to assuage the anxiety of not knowing where you're headed or what's ahead.

When I wrapped up my sessions, reflecting with my self, by my self became my therapy. And after more journaling and more self-reflection, I discovered that my "problem" to overcome, per se, was not to actualize my ability or willingness to move forward and take up space in the world, but rather strengthen my belief in my self and in the Universe to make space for me – especially in moments when my path did not seem as straightforward or wide open. And that required a different level of vulnerability to better understand why.

"That's Not My Name!"

At some point during that time, I remember taking an Uber ride with a driver named Ubaka, who offered me some advice:

- Focus on your education, doing the next thing. Then find a partner who matches similar goals to you.
- You can do anything you put your mind to – it doesn't matter if you're a female, you're a person first (*I have some thoughts about this reading this four years later, but I digress*).

41

- Have soul, everything comes from the soul. God gives to us from the soul and we give to others from our soul.
- Life is about healthy competition and (emotional) discipline.
- Something about Muhammad Ali.
- Don't do dirty politics.
- Everything is a product of your focus – Commit to an idea of the thing you want to manifest, then the Universe will move around it to make it happen for you.

I'm not sure if there was a through-line or point of cohesion among any of these pieces of advice, but somehow they all individually and collectively resonated with me. There's something to be said about the way God can truly speak through Uber drivers who just feel inclined to put you on game just because you're in the space to hear it.

Another thing Ubaka told me during that Uber ride actually impacted me pretty heavily in a way that I didn't expect. "Your name…in Ghana, it's used to refer to a big or important person. Someone who is larger than life." In his Ghanaian accent, it sounded like "Keh-sih." I later learned that this definition comes from the Akuapem dialect of Akan Twi.

The meaning of my name that I was previously familiar with was the Swahili definition, which means "lawsuit" or "child born while father was in hard times" which isn't the reason I was named that nor is it in any way special or significant. My parents simply found the name in an African baby name book and wanted to name me something that looked African but still sounded American. I always thought they should have spelled it "Casey" which would've also fit in our family better – since their names both start with "C." It also would've been less of a struggle for people to pronounce – but I digress.

I think on the surface, it shouldn't seem like that big of a deal, right? My name is different, I get it. But there's something about the first time someone addresses you, or whenever you're called on and there is attention on you, it's associated with a mistake.

People made it a joke because they didn't know how to pronounce it. The fact that people rarely know how to pronounce it makes me feel exposed under the circumstance of a mistake. If I was just given another name, I wouldn't feel like a mistake.

My name was never difficult to pronounce now that I think about it, it was just different. My Kesi wasn't like anybody else's Casey or Kasey or KC. I remember a firefighter – a Black man – calling me Keisha when handing out the certificates of completion from our fourth-grade fire safety training. Countless substitute teachers mispronounced my name during roll call, ruining the streak of it not being mispronounced after my teachers finally learned it following the first days of school.

I couldn't really shorten my already-short name. I wasn't creative enough to come up with a nickname. So I was stuck with Kesi.

I wish I cared often enough to be firm or direct to correct

people when they mispronounce it. I pretty much assume that it's always going to be some bullshit whenever someone acknowledges me by my name. It's gotten better as I've gotten older. My name isn't what some might consider "ghetto-sounding" to warrant caution that it might cost me whatever opportunities an employer might've denied another Black person with a less "white-sounding" name. But it's different enough to have always made me feel othered.

And even as I'm writing, I realize that I don't even have that much of a problem with my name. I don't have a problem with my parents over the name they chose for me. I have a problem with the lack of care and intention that others have given to my name and, by default, me as a person. People were careless with it. There was no desire to ask how to pronounce it before fumbling through any version of Kessie or Keesie or Kelsie. There was no desire to read my email address or signature before mistyping it in their reply. Now that I think about it, there's a certain erasure of the self that happens when your name is constantly mispronounced or misspelled. It's a feeling of who you are, who you see and understand your self to be, being eroded right in front of you. And people just carry on right after.

These days, when people make an intentional effort to learn my name and pronounce it correctly, even to add my little accent (which *technically* isn't on my official government documents but I add it for a little spicé), I notice, and it matters. I won't say it's super significant, because that should be the bare minimum of addressing Black people – or any person of color's name for that matter – with respect. I also realized that as I expect that regard from others, I also should offer that same regard to other people and their names. Because it's the bare minimum.

After learning the meaning of my name in Twi, I realized that I focused more on the fact that people mispronounced it. Like I said, I'm rarely quick to correct people if they do mispronounce it, and I've also never wondered if there was another meaning than the one I initially learned about. I remained attached to the first thing I was told about my name – that it was insignificant, that the intentional balance of both African and American was insignificant. I internalized that fact as a determination of my own insignificance.

My name is one very clear illustration of how I've allowed other people's perception of me to be the first and final, that these are the people that I believed knew me so well to have so much say. People who've known me for only a moment but whom I give so much unspoken permission to speak so much over me. It was certainly a contributing factor to my subconscious goal in life to keep my head down and just stay in the lines, show up where I was expected to show up, and not be seen or heard.

I think the idealized version of my self I had in my head was mainly just about being someone who people regarded highly and took seriously. That one voice changed my entire perception of and feelings about my name...and really my self. It illuminated the fact that my desire to avoid being seen can be traced back to my relationship with my name. About how some might say it's weird or different or hard to pronounce, about how that fact is often an imposition to any space I occupy and prevents me from being able to just blend in and not stick out.

That one Uber ride changed my entire perspective of my name and how I felt about it, and really my self. "If I was just given a different name, I wouldn't be addressed with a mistake with every first introduction."

However, the shifting moment for me was the realization that I didn't have to place so much value on others' expectations just because that was the first and loudest thing I was offered. Contrary to what I believed before, I could decide for my self who and how I wanted to be in this life. The potential of self-determination opened a door of curiosity that I wasn't told even existed before, but I was nonetheless still eager to begin the journey to dig deeper into the infinite possibilities of who I could be and what experience in this world.

Who told you you were naked?… Who taught you to hate your self?

Being disconnected from our ancestry and heritage, not really feeling connected to African culture in a way that makes me feel like it truly belongs to me. It feels like I'm borrowing it or renting it out but in reality, I know that at the end of the day I have to hang it up and return to my own heritage – one that I've been led to believe is damaged and broken and irredeemable. Almost like the idea and possibility of me becoming something or someone greater than I currently am – I feel open to cosplaying it, but don't feel like I can truly transform or evolve into it permanently. So you experience that alignment in moments, never a gradual shift into something that seems like it could last forever. It's really hard to imagine your self, your world, your way of being as something different and genuinely believe that you have the power to not only ground that imagining in reality but manifest it. It's easier to be complacent with how things are and feel defeated by the false belief that life as it currently exists cannot be radically different.

Black Americans are stuck with a collective memory of pain and struggle, and the further back we go the less access we have to our history as it has been deliberately erased or is too painful to want to remember. But the good parts that we have to celebrate and rejoice in, get lost too. And then we are left with a false narrative about our lives and our history, which has more likely than not been written by someone else.

When other people would speak that life into me, my instinct was to not believe it simply because I didn't think they "knew me" well enough to make any type of judgment of me – positive or negative. Because the people that have known me and been around me longer feel another way about me, so their perspective must be the truth, right?

Either way, I try to take it all with a grain of salt, and I'm learning to remember that my opinion of my self is paramount. The way I've navigated the world up until this point has privileged other people with the authority to set the goalposts for who and how I should be in the world. That bar is seemingly always moving and more often than not wouldn't speak to my innermost desires – the things that tug at my spirit incessantly but that I can't yet name – anyways.

The way I am truly meant to show up in the world will take years of life to cultivate – I believe the essence is there, though. At my core. So now it's about digging. Digging the diamond that is your authentic self out of a seemingly insurmountable mound of other's perspectives, built up over a lifetime.

Also, I'm learning to shatter the idea that I have to be or do one specific thing in life and remain married to it. Although I haven't yet experienced it, I understand that the more I live, learn and evolve, a particular way of being may no longer speak to who I am in a given moment. I have to cultivate a sense of self-knowledge and connection to my intuition to feel that separation – of who I am presenting to be and where my higher self is trying to go – in your spirit. Without that, the feeling sits there unknowingly as I move aimlessly through the world, or I'll deny it – privileging safety, familiarity, and comfort – as a more blatant act of betrayal. To my self and the people I belong to.

Many of those serendipitous moments in those Ubers confirmed my path and helped me to rethink my perspective of and belief in my self. Certain people and events in your life will leave you with ideas about your self that create and solidify a disempowering narrative. And someone else comes along to speak life over you, or share a simple act of kindness, they ultimately upend all of that in one conversation without ever knowing you. Those singular moments have the potential to breathe more life into you and where you have the potential to go, instead of leaving you feeling trapped with whoever or wherever you are in the moment.

A lot of the way we speak to each other is based on who we've made each other up to be in our heads without taking the time to truly be present and get to know one another – our fears, desires, interests, passions, quirks – or we trap them within limiting social stereotypes and ideas of who we believe they can be.

I hate the idea that some people can tell you about your self your whole life, people who claim to know you so well, about your weird, less desirable parts. People who've known you for but a moment speak so much life into you.

* * *

As someone who is raised in the Black middle class – there's a very thin line when it comes to prioritizing material security and access to a point where you begin to inch too close to the line and even go as far as to threaten it. when that happens, your internal alarm goes off. you try to convince your self and others to step back from that ledge.

It's too easy to teeter the line and sway too far one way or the other depending on how discomforting the issue at hand is. We see that happen often with broader sociopolitical issues, but I would also argue that it plays a much bigger role in how we understand and navigate identity exploration and individuation.

49

- Being bucked up to have big aspirations, but not being made to feel like I was capable of actually achieving that based on who I am, being successfully responsible for my life based on who I am
- Fear about safety and security – needing to make sure your doors are locked at night in your quiet suburban home
- What is the genuine meaning of safety and stability? Insulating your self from the world – in your world, among that which is familiar – hoping that will protect you, but life will life anyway – change and evolution will happen anyway. New parts of you that you didn't know or recognize or acknowledge will find you whether or not you account for it.

Black middle-class ideals include getting your education, finding a good job, and more than likely starting a family. That doesn't mean you're actually taught how to get to know your self and what you want. You're just doing what you think it takes to create a good life – I don't think about it, just follow the script.

Self-exploration felt like a black-and-white binary of (uncritically settling for the first idea of who and how I have to be in the world) and (separating all together and abandoning or rejecting a world that I don't have a complete issue with)

I responded to this by avoiding exploration of my self, but I also wasn't sure if I was 100% happy and at peace. If I was truly secure and clear about who I was and was becoming, and if that was the "right" – or even what that meant.

The phrase "You have to work twice as hard to get half of what they have" was popularized by *Scandal*. While it does encapsulate what the world tells Black people is required for success – it also centers white people and white standards of success as our bar in the first place.

> *"One thread of thinking in the African American community holds that these depressing numbers partially stem from cultural pathologies that can be altered through individual grit and exceptionally good behavior. (In 2011, Philadelphia Mayor Michael Nutter, responding to violence among young black males, put the blame on the family: "Too many men making too many babies they don't want to take care of, and then we end up dealing with your children." Nutter turned to those presumably fatherless babies: "Pull your pants up and buy a belt, because no one wants to see your underwear or the crack of your butt.") The thread is as old as black politics itself. It is also wrong. The kind of trenchant racism to which black people have persistently been subjected can never be defeated by making its victims more respectable. The essence of American racism is disrespect. And in the wake of the grim numbers, we see the grim inheritance." – Ta-Nehisi Coates, The Case for Reparations*[12]

I don't always want to or have to hustle. I don't have to work twice as hard. I don't want to have to be hypervigilant about my behavior and my appearance. I don't want to do any of that because it's rooted in an incessant concern with the white gaze. I don't care to participate in that.

I am exceptional, I know that, but why? It can't be from living and dreaming based on the standards everybody else set before me.

It makes it easy to follow a predetermined blueprint without doing the inner work, especially when that blueprint is laid out and informed by broader cultural and familial expectations. It feels easy to want to say because of certain material accomplishments for the potential for those accomplishments – especially given my social positioning in the world. But I've spent the entirety of this book – and in real-world time, the past five years – grappling with why that is not and cannot be enough.

When working to unpack the source of these internal narratives, I realized that they have less to do with me being personally hard on my self. Through my learning and research, I came to understand that much of this internal narrative is actually a cultural one – one that has told Black people for centuries about the limits, deficits, and gaps in who we are and what we are capable of. That we have to work "twice as hard" for "half as much." Although I used to hate how often people repeated that phrase because we all got it from Scandal, the experiences it represents are generational.

Those experiences have placed us collectively within a stark power dynamic with white supremacist capitalist patriarchy. This dynamic tells us constantly, in all aspects of our culture, that our only way to being "enough" is through the institutions and systems they created that only reinforce that power dynamic rather than attempt to balance it.

In my experience, this is particularly true when it comes to our names, our spirituality, our image, our achievements, our culture, and our power.

The Cassius Clays become Muhammad Alis, the Independence Days become Juneteenth Jubilees, and white evangelicalism instead becomes an opportunity for deeper interrogation and Black resistance.

Previous generations of Black people want us to be fine upholding the status quo instead of doing the extra leg work to truly heal, imagine, and build a new world.

I want to accept the invitation to step out of the constraints of what we're told we can be to who we actually are – to actually address the root causes and aim for holistic solutions and deeper healing. To understand that it is an internal battle as much as it is a battle of engaging with current systems to dismantle them.

As I've continued to explore these ideas, as well as my own personal journey, I realize that the point of it all is less about pursuing what you know will be the discovery of a certain, better, more empowering outcome – whether that's in regards to my personal destiny or with regards to the conditions of Blackness in America.

I feel as though the point of it all is meant to be an invitation to think about the possibility of the answer to the question of "Who am I?" and "Who am I meant to be?" being different than what I was made to believe. I see it as an opportunity to explore one's potential in a different way – not just in a way that is solely about the pursuit of the outcome itself, but in a way that instead challenges the premise of who gets to decide and define whose potential.

* * *

During another Uber ride I took during my freshman year of college (it seems like my Uber rides have always come with the occasional synchronicity, but this was the OG one) – the driver offered some advice that stuck with me (and by "stuck with me," I mean I immediately wrote it down in my notes app and it's been there ever since):

> *"Don't worry about money or a husband. Worry about your education because no one can take away your education." – D. (Uber Driver)*

He was talking to me about how he and his friends made a lot of money in the country they were from but came to America. He came and raised a daughter, whom he said I reminded him of. He said that the money he makes from Uber and other work he gives to his wife and daughter and then the other half he uses to buy basketball sneakers to send back to his home country. I did wonder to my self, "If you all made a lot of money in your own country, why leave?" I wish I heard what country he is actually from because my next thought was that America does free people of a lot of political turmoil that occurs in other countries but I didn't want to make that assumption without proper context...But the thing that struck me most was that he never mentioned saving his money for himself. He gives it all to his family and back to his country. He also gave me other fatherly advice like reminding me to study and not worry about boys. He said to really work and focus on my education while I'm young because it's harder once you're older. "You remind me a lot of my daughter so that's why I'm telling you all of this," he said.

This means so much to me now because of course being in a new place in school I constantly wonder if it's worth it or if it will pay off. You wonder about your own success at the end of all of this. In reality, all of it is futile if, at the end of the day, you aren't helping other people. If you aren't using your experiences to pass on to those coming after you to make it a little easier for them. College isn't going to be easy, but it will definitely be worth it. Invest in your self and your education now so that you can reap the most benefits later on and use that to better serve your community.

I've never desired to really be seen, I think that's an ego-boosting perk of doing good work, but I know that my true desire is for my energy to be undeniably felt. Reflecting on these rides reminds me to not be overly skeptical when people speak life into me and to not take other people's criticisms as fact. However, it does remind me to listen when their feedback is rooted in a genuine desire for me to do better and comes from those who know me and care about me, and who see the best in me. Those who reflect back to me my positive potential.

I don't think there's any singular handful of redeeming qualities that make me more exceptional than other people that are new under the Sun.

I believe it's just because I have relentlessly pursued full acknowledgment and embodiment of my humanity, and have worked to be incredibly honest, yet compassionate, with my self about the barriers that have prevented me (and still prevent me) from reaching that aim.

However, I want to learn how to remove the noise and remember that I have the answers within me already. I want to learn to trust my intuition and inner voice more and designate my self – rather than any external entity – as the authority of my life.

And when God wants you to hear and be more attuned to that voice, you'll hear it. They will intercept in the most simple of ways to confirm the path you're already on, or invite you to step onto a greater one.

Take Me To The Water

"See that band all dressed in white
God is gonna trouble these waters...
My Lord delivered Daniel well
Daniel well, Daniel well
Didn't my Lord deliver Daniel well
Then why not every man?"
– Wade in the Water, Negro Spiritual

"As water wears away stones and torrents wash away
the soil, so you destroy man's hope. You overpower him
once for all, and he is gone; you change his countenance
and send him away." – Job 14:19-22

I think this is a story about salvation. But what does salvation even mean? To me?

My idea of Heaven would be a quiet beach or in the middle of the ocean. Somewhere where I can be gently reminded of how small I am, in the midst of the world's expansiveness. Where I can experience a quiet and isolated existence.

Where you know that heaven is not something to be earned or created or fought for, it just is. Where peace and solace are your birthright.

Where I know I always have access to grace and the potential of a new beginning.

My idea of salvation is a place where things are quiet and easy and simple. It's a place where it's tranquil, where I can feel and see endless possibilities. Where I don't feel immediately called or moved to act, where it's okay to sit with that feeling and in that space.

My idea of salvation is being grounded in the knowing that while I'm here – during this life – I want to spend my time and energy seeking peace and alignment with my self and God and the Universe, rather than trying to avoid perceived failure and chaos.

* * *

Although I technically didn't "grow up in the church" it is absolutely a major part of my identity as a Black woman from the South.

I guess that would make me a Cultural Christian – not one that cosplays as a Christian, but who, funny enough, is in it but not of it.

While I didn't grow up having a church home of my own, I was still connected to churches by way of my extended family and close friends.

I appreciated the music, the oration, the messages in the sermons. It was and still is deeply and inextricably tied to how I made sense of a broader cultural identity within the Black community.

Before college, I decided to get baptized, and in college, I discovered a church home (by way of friends), started attending regularly on my own, got more involved with the production team, and attended community events.

Finding and cultivating my own relationship with God and with the church for my self helped me at a time when I needed to be anchored in something bigger than my self and my immediate world.

At one point I lived across the street from a church in D.C. and visited in passing once. That particular Sunday, they were doing baptisms, and singing the traditional Negro Spiritual Take Me to the Water.

Hearing that for the first time gave me the feeling of being connected to my history and being grounded in faith that has more weight than a typical "Performance Church."

* * *

It's interesting to me how throughout history, the Black church has been a site of personal and collective liberation. A place for meetings during the Civil Rights Movement, a hiding place for enslaved folks as they made their way North to freedom. A place for individual revelation and renewal.

Yet and still, the Black church has also been another stage on which people perform their ego and their commitment to respectability politics and intracommunal violence.

You're not praising loud enough – so is that why people hoot and holler like that? Why they fall out and speak in tongues? When I feel the Holy Spirit I just get overwhelmed and cry, is that okay?

Your neighbor only tolerates you – at best, they only make space for the acceptable parts of you. At worst, they enact the same types of oppression as your enemy out there in the world. But you have to love them as your self, right?

The church offers a gateway to an intergenerational connection to older Black folks who went through and have been through some shit, who have an actual testimony. How do you begin to cultivate that as a young person simply navigating uncertainty about who I am and my place in the world?

Longing for the promises of life and salvation becomes not about escapism but about romanticizing. Adding magic and romance to an otherwise boring and outright painful existence.

The learned helplessness and hopelessness lead us to double down on faith, hope, and resilience. We tell our selves to "renew our minds" and give thanks for the goodness we do have and have experienced. To not be too greedy for more goodness or to mute our desires for more goodness altogether.

Bittersweet, how sorrow and longing somehow make us feel whole and connected.

* * *

There is a cultural directive that says "Whatever you do, don't tell the truth about what it's like to be alive."

We explicitly and implicitly tell each other to avoid the reality of negative emotions and uncertainty and things being out of our control. To be afraid of the truth of who you are and what you want out of this life on Earth.

To avoid facing the truth of how you feel about your self and your life by maintaining a posture of constant hope and optimism.

What happens if I'm honest with God (other people, my self) about my feeling of loneliness and isolation, after being crushed under certain expectations? What if I was honest about my negative emotions and feelings?

So then maybe that is the extent of my ability to be honest with my self and, because I know God is listening, it's the extent of my stability in my relationship with God, too.

How do you hold space for your self, other people, God – when you feel like you're being forgotten?

* * *

I'd be lying if I said that there wasn't a part of me that feels like all of this is a punishment for hoping and dreaming. For flying too close to the Sun.

I'd be lying if I said I didn't have fear and anxiety related to the possibility of stepping into new identities and roles with increased levels of responsibility. I fear being overwhelmed or engulfed by my experiences. I'm afraid that who I might become won't be familiar to me anymore.

I am angry about the fact that no one has told me what to do or who to be. That I have to create her from scratch. I have nothing to rebel against. No prescribed destiny to dispute. Like everyone else on this rock we call Earth, no manual or guide to help me figure out the journey. At times, that has left me feeling overwhelmed by the complexity of life and the fact that it's so big with so many different possibilities and ways to experience it. I have to reckon with the fact that I can't live all of those experiences at once (or at all), but I can choose to show up in the fullness of who God has called me to be in every phase of my life. I can choose who I get to be and live as large or small a life as I please. I can choose to utilize the wealth of information this world has to offer to inform my decisions and set the foundation for a life that exudes love, impact, and legacy. And the best part is, I don't need anyone's permission to do it.

There are times to swim against the current and times along the current. Surrendering and swimming along does not have to equal laziness and giving up your power.

Even though I'm much better positioned to build the life that I truly need and desire from a healthy and mature place I still have to sit with and process the grief that the dream as I once knew it doesn't exist anymore.

This feeling is not a thing to be fixed or hidden or painted over with Psalms and positive affirmations.

In Paulo Coelho's *The Alchemist*, there's a part that deeply resonated with me: "My Heart Is Afraid that it will have to suffer."

I'm familiar with discomfort, but I recognize that I have a deep fear of true suffering. Emotionally, physically, mentally, and spiritually.

I think I am also afraid of stagnancy and the idea of not

reaching my full potential, but also a fear of reaching past comfort and potentially suffering. Living passively versus intuitively and in surrender to whatever higher path might be meant for me.

I think that I deal with fear with mental hypervigilance – masking my anxiety around a lack of existential control with a desire to care and be of service to things bigger than my self to the extent of self-betrayal.

Specifically, that's how I deal with the fear of/from watching people or my self suffer and feeling like I can't do anything about it. From no wanting other people to feel alone or left behind or unacknowledged and uncared for. But then I am forced to realize the limitations of that because I'm only one person and I am a human being.

This hyper-sense of control is meant to combat and convince my self that I have some semblance of it, even though I know, deep down, I am powerless in the grand scheme of things. Powerlessness over other people and entities – especially those that were here before me that impact how I'm perceived and treated.

It subconsciously reinforces that the only way to get what I want and need – the only way to be cared for – means I have to put in an inordinate amount of energy and effort, or take up space and resources from other people. I've struggled with the idea of being that person – so it instead made more sense put that effort into making my self small and easy to deal with. For my self, and other people.

Journal – undated

Control issues, fear of letting go

Lack of trust in God, the Universe, in other people

A false sense of independence and self-reliance

If I don't do the work then everything will fall apart → Let it fall apart, what happens then?

Fear of that idea of the unknown – you want to control everything to be able to figure everything out and understand it so that you can maintain the false sense of safety and security because it makes you feel more comfortable when moving forward.

When you go through a series of disappointments, a part of me feels like the Universe is saying, loudly and clearly, that you don't deserve good things. I've learned that you can want something really badly – you can pray for it, wish for it, set all of your intentions and energy towards it – and still not receive it. This series of disappointments leave the ego feeling disheartened and let down. Maybe this was all the result of me feeling entitled to various outcomes, most notably because deep down I felt like I was a good person, so good things should happen to me... I should get what I want.

The Ego – my ego rather – wants me to be in a constant state of anxiety and unknowing. It wants me to go to extreme measures to ensure I have control of every situation. It causes me to believe I am unsafe because of the natural fact that we can't possibly know every outcome in our lives. It doesn't want me to experience peaceful, calm energy. It wants me to be passive, afraid, and meek.

My Ego wants me to believe that I am not deserving of good things. So when my circumstances don't meet my expectations, it only confirms that and leaves me feeling like my lack of value is the cause (or even the result) of things not going my way. This, coupled with inaction and passive longing, almost ensures the things I desire most will never come to fruition.

My Ego, while I'm in the midst of working on various projects (such as this book) uses the little voice in my head to tell me that no one cares about my work, that I am unimportant, not valuable, and not impactful. Despite when people tell me otherwise, my overpowering ego is attuned to negativity and actively seeking things within the Universe to nurture and fortify it.

Social media is a great example of one of my Ego's favorite places. When posts don't receive the likes I expected, when people don't engage as much with a post I thought slapped, the ego is right there to remind me that I am not important, my content is not good, and that I should stop posting. And then it feeds on my insecurities by pushing me to shitpost even more in the quest for more digital attention. My philosophy towards social media now is that I know my Instagram pictures are not the best, I just like it as a platform to share pictures of my favorite memories. I know that joke I thought was funny or would get retweets on Twitter wasn't successful, but it resonated with me and I liked the post, so I published it. The point here is not how (or if) other people receive it the way I want them to, the point is that I should feel confident and happy with the content I produce. My only goal through my social media is to spread positivity, enlightenment and joy through my socials. When I lose sight of that, it becomes a playground for my Ego.

The main lesson I'm learning even as I write this is that it's not about what the outcome is or how other people receive it. I am no longer pressed to control the outcome of situations or to control other people's perceptions of me. What I can do is be firmly rooted in who I am and be her unapologetically, not allowing this fickle world to force her into her shell.

Non-attachment – the belief that the outcomes I desire are possible, without the unnecessary attachment to them ("If this doesn't happen the way I want it to, I will be okay. I am no less of a person...no less valuable, capable, or deserving. Abundance in wealth and love are always flowing from and to me.)

Who am I at my highest self? What does she believe in? How does she carry her self? How does she treat and love her self? How does she treat and love others? How does she compete? How does she win and fail?

My desire to be and become feels very fragile right now. Who is all of this effort really for?

What if I put all this effort into becoming, then lose it, or have it taken away from me?

I want to expedite the process of self-discovery and revelation. I want to get to the part where I feel more worthy of being chosen or favored. More worthy of salvation.

Instead of these shallow and empty expectations, I want to have a sense of hope and faith that is anchored and aligned with the truth of who I am and who I want to be and become.

What do you want? You can't answer that question without knowing who you are, you can't be afraid that the truth of who you are might align with something that the world says doesn't deserve good things.

I think I bypass wanting anything good for my self to want and work for better futures for people who look like me and share my identities or experiences. I'm beginning to think it's okay to reframe that and say that I want good things for my self, too. It's okay to want good things for my self in this lifetime.

What does it even mean for me to feel fulfilled in life? I think that positioning that as a question allows more open space for me to feel grounded in where I am right now and explore what might be possible. Rather than definitively stating that I am unhappy that there is something that needs to be fixed or changed when that really isn't the case.

I think the suffering and the disconnection come from automatically assuming that it is impossible to already have the things that you need to feel content, and simultaneously being uncritical or unintentional about your life, and just assuming that you're happy and rolling with the punches so as to not be unnecessarily negative or contrarian.

Maybe I am afraid of the possibility that I may not have what it takes to simply be fully present with my life with all that it may be asking of me at this moment. Maybe I want to outsource responsibility to someone or something else, or to the future at some unspecified time in space, to give my self more time to prepare or get ready. To acquire whatever characteristics or skills or knowledge I believe I don't already possess.

Notes – August 17, 2022

On spiritual bypassing:

Remember: You're human and sometimes (a lot of times) shit is hard

Keep your head down and stay focused. Don't be afraid to hold space for your self to feel your feelings, don't be afraid to ask for help and seek out support with getting basic human emotional needs met. Trust that people will show up for you when you communicate and give them room to show up for you.

Ego death (death of the victim and perfectionist mindsets due to fear of lacking control) – I want to take care of everyone else because I wasn't given that same treatment. It's a valid response that served me in order to help me "survive," but it has left me, in this moment, paralyzed with fear at the thought of leaving everything behind in order to become who I know I'm meant to be.

Goal: move beyond habitual patterns of self-abandonment

How do I practice showing up for my own needs? Start by

acknowledging the ways in which I historically have not shown up for my self and my physical, mental, and spiritual needs.

Previous attempts at self-reliance were not genuine because they were rooted in a limiting story of not needing other people, or in the belief that I could work and think my way out of disappointment.

Feel, acknowledge, and come to terms with the disappointment that comes from not being totally in control.

Mami Wata

I recently learned about Mami Wata, the water spirit venerated in African spirituality, and the Kalunga line – a watery boundary between the world of the living and the dead in religious traditions of the Congo region. It's also represented in African spirituality – specifically Bakongo spirituality – as the water boundary between Earth and the ancestral realm.

With that, I think often about the enslaved Africans who would jump into the ocean to drown rather than take on an identity and life that was forced on them. About the generations that followed who view water as a source for renewal. For hope.

Sometimes hope and optimism feel counterproductive to me – harmful even. Like it would be more beneficial to force my self to sit with reality, and the fact that I may not achieve my dreams and hopes and wishes for my life. There may actually not be some grand divine plan being carried out by some higher power for my benefit and favor.

It feels futile to put in the work to be so positive and hopeful about the things I want in life when I feel like it might not matter to God or the Universe at the end of the day.

Your story may not have a happy ending after all. It may actually end very badly, or maybe – because of your (relative) insignificance to the Universe – your story may just end.

It may turn out that you are actually just a bag of meat and bones just living and moving through life to check boxes, and once your checklist of a life is complete, it's over. And that is it.

How do you respond when you don't get the happy ending you fixated your energy on? Who do you become as a result of a bruised ego and a broken heart?

I know that mentality makes you passive because, at the end of the day, you feel like you don't have a choice in your fate, so why bother?

There's a balance of acceptance and surrender to what is, and grief for what was or what you hoped for (the good, bad, and familiar). There's also room for giving your self permission to want and hope for and look forward to – lean into and embrace – the good that is to come and that is currently available to you.

There's a part of me that wants to let it all fall apart. A part of me that is curious about the potential of chaos brought on by facing the unknown. What if I didn't force my hand either way? What if I allowed room for fate to simply be? Where could my current path take me? I know that I'd be okay that things would be okay, but there is an underlying worry about the specifics of how.

It feels like I'm sitting on the precipice of chaos and complacency. I'm not choosing chaos but I also wouldn't mind if it just…happened.

Journal – May 13, 2019

I've been here – physically present – but lacked purpose and focus. Analogy: Floating around through life with nothing anchoring you down – family, God, a destination. That gives me anxiety because it's so easy to get caught up in everything going on around me, without that focus of being 100% clear on what I'm doing here and where I'm going. And for who.

Who am I? What is my worth if not for who I might one day become?

Subconsciously I didn't feel I was good enough to be and have what I wanted in life – so I made it about fixing or working on my self.

That by trying to convince God that I was a good person and that I stay in the lines – I'll get good karma. Salvation.

Because They say that all I had to do was be born and exist

to be riddled with sin and the baggage of identities I did not willingly choose. Right?

They say that there are dire consequences if I don't do the right thing, if I fail. That to fail and suffer and be disappointed must somehow be your fault, because of something you did or didn't do.

So, if I avoid feelings of failure (real or imagined) or skirt past them by not fully engaging with my feelings about failure publicly, I won't have to acknowledge that there might be something inherent in me that leads to the inevitable failure. Right?

If I can be honest, sometimes I feel like I am going through the motions of a life that I don't necessarily feel connected to.

Sometimes that feels easier than being actively engaged – easier than feeling everything and questioning instincts that feel as though they come as easy as breathing. but I think most of all – being actively engaged would force me to be honest about the fact that while I recognize that my life is good, great even, as it is – a fully realized life still takes time and effort to build. And I want the freedom to be honest about the fact that I often wonder if that time and effort is and will be worth it.

It's a constant feeling of – not necessarily sadness (at least I don't think) – but a heaviness, from constantly evaluating the weight of my life. Maybe it's anxiety. An uncomfortable humming. Always present. Something that can't be thought away, motivational quote'd away, self-help book'ed away, "just something to take the edge off"ed away.

Knowing the potential answer or solution or ending to the story doesn't change the truth of how I feel right now. I don't know if I currently have access to the energy and willpower to understand what changes need to happen in my life. The frustration that is caused by that is maddening.

I wasn't shown how to truly feel disappointment, grief, or lack of faith openly and in an embodied way; without the need to rush in to fix it or make it feel better or convince my self of some other more positive feeling.

Faith was a tool to help me make it make sense, to help me make meaning out of abstract emotions and experiences to be able to move forward and grow – but once it stopped making sense, and I had nowhere else to go but inward.

* * *

I don't want to be stuck in a place (or story) mentally or emotionally that I'm no longer in. I don't want to feel held down by other people's baggage. I give my self permission to release (and be released) from the limiting and negative stories in my mind, so that I can make room for other things.

What if you slowed down and paid attention to where life is inviting you to grow, expand, and learn? What if you learned to slow down and give your self credit for the knowledge and skills that you already have that are waiting to be embodied?

What if you recognized that the way you've operated can be self-limiting and that in order to make room for a higher version of your self, you'd have to let go but compassionately and with gratitude for how far that version of my self got you?

* * *

Letter to my self – undated

Hey, Kés.

Before we get to the end of this decade I want to take a moment to thank you. To honor you. But most importantly, to let you know that I see you.

You think this boy, this opportunity, this way of life is the gatekeeper to that which you most desire, so you smile your way out of authenticity and silence your way out of emotional honesty, all to maintain an illusion of security because God forbid they know the real you.

What may be only slightly worse than the mask you cling so desperately to, is the false belief you hold with it that no one can tell it's a mask.

I won't lie, learning how to fully be in the world will be a lifelong journey, one that I have yet to master, one that will keep you in a constant battle between fully stepping into who you've always known you are and crumbling under the perceived pressure of others' expectations.

The lesson of my life has been that we have always known. What you know to be true about your self is what I wish I trusted my self enough to believe.

This world will attempt to pacify that desire within you that believes that better is always possible. You will be made to feel like the dreams you have for your self in this life are meant to stay dreams, fantasies – the sole purpose of which are to make the life you settle for a little less miserable.

You think other people navigate the world with much more ease than you do and for whatever reason, you feel like that same quality does not apply to you. This "secret sauce" to life does not exist. Maintaining this belief will keep you in an endless search for something outside of your self. Never satisfied, always restless.

The moment you realize that the answers you search so desperately for are within you will begin to see what truly matters in this life and that you hold the power to manifest that which has always belonged to you.

Never let this life weigh you down, Don't forfeit your power to a world that is committed to chaos and wedded to ego. Despite this, remember that your purpose is to help people and create dope shit. Do that in whatever way is meaningful to you and know that, at the end of the day, none of this is about you. Yes, the goal is to complete your divine assignment, but understand that the purpose of your time on Earth is to provide you with the experiences and relationships that will catalyze your growth and facilitate your ability to enjoy the simple pleasures in life.

This will seem superfluous at times, but allowing your self to fully be human and enjoy being in the world, especially as you continue to occupy the identity of Black womanhood, is inextricably connected to your mission, should you choose to accept it. Don't run your self ragged trying to sow the seeds that you deny your self the chance to reap the fruits of your labor.

You fear responsibility and want to maintain your childlike wonder of the world. You deny your self the opportunity to cultivate true confidence and power this way. The fuck ups you fear and try so desperately to avoid are inevitable, you know. Your fear of looking silly and, more important, incompetent and inexperienced is, at its root, the fear of your own self-actualization.

You fear not only fucking up but doing so where other people can see you. Because God forbid people know that you're human. The quality that will serve you best in this life is the ability to admit what you don't know. No one is expecting you to, that's what this journey called life is for. I don't believe we'd suffer so much if that were the case.

Always remember that you have much to learn in this life, young Padawan. The answers to the questions you seek will not be handed to you on a silver platter. You must find them buried underneath your life experiences. Quiet the noise of external expectations and more importantly your harshest critic, your self. Your will to exceed your own standards will carry you through this life, into rooms you could never imagine you'd be in. But never forget how far you've come, and that you've barely scratched the surface of your potential. Grace is always available, you just have to loosen your grip on your life and allow it to come to you.

*　*　*

Are you genuinely happy with the person that you are and are becoming?

It's okay if in some areas of your life, the answer is no. It can invite an opportunity to see where you can be more intentional and focused, and where you can be more accepting and gracious.

I acknowledge that sometimes it feels like all the good things might be gone by Sunrise. And the pain of being honest about my disappointment with how certain aspects of life have turned out this far. And the grief associated with that. And the shame of feeling like I shouldn't feel disappointed. Does God care that I am hurt and disappointed?

There are some things about my life that I am grieving, and other things that I am awaiting their emergence. I feel this way because I care about my life and my fleeting time. I want to get it right the first time, so I can just do the work I am here to do and move on.

It's not about perfection for perfection's sake, but I do have to heal my relationship with the Universe and with time – and my self – because we are in conflict.

To be exactly the person I am meant to be and become, I want to find a balance of being connected enough that I feel responsible to and for something, but not diving in so deep that I crumble under pressure.

I acknowledge that I want things to work and be right because it I feel like having to double back to clean up your mistakes wastes time. But I guess it's about allowing your self grace to become. I guess that making mistakes is just part of being human, and that being human is the whole point. Allowing your self space to be human is the point.

The world is very big, and I feel very small, but that doesn't scare me anymore. It's deeply humbling in a way that allows me to just say and take all of that in and begin the attempt to orient my self to how I want to fit into it.

God I know loves me and has a greater plan. I think it's the Universe that I struggle to trust – the forces of nature, other human beings operating in their free will, and the impacts of my social positioning in the world as a young Black woman. That is what I feel I'm up against, that is the insurmountable force that I fear will keep me from being and becoming the person I dream of.

Honor and respect the journey God has for me by not rushing or forcing it. Honor and respect the journey God has for me by not being pressed over needing to know and have control over the details of how it will all unfold.

There may have been experiences that have caused you to lose trust in the ground underneath your feet and its ability to carry you from one moment to the next. I get it. but what you do have, and what you have always had, is your essence.

But this expectation or idea that you're supposed to have that level of control in the input – and more specifically the outputs – of your life is unsustainable.

To believe that you can be and do everything and everywhere at once is not only impossible is arrogant. It shows that you don't trust your self, the Universe, God, other people... life, to show up for you.

What *is* in your power is to do the work to get clear on your self, your inner voice, and your choices, values, needs, and wants; to become secure in who you've been this far and what she's experienced, and the lessons that she's learned and is learning.

Get clear and secure and your essence. The body, the personality, the job or career, the money, the relationships, the interests, and the hobbies – can and will change and evolve. But you will always be and have your essence. Protect it.

When you're clear on who you are and what you're about, you have more peace of mind without fear of how things will turn out. You get more open, and there is so much more possibility in openness – in leading life with curiosity rather than expectation.

I no longer have the energy to fight a losing battle against fate anymore. If it's meant to fall apart at my feet, let it. What if I just let everything fall apart?

I can't repair my relationship with my life and the Universe if I don't trust it to make space for me.

Surrender. Because you know nothing. Allow God to carry you to shore instead of swimming forcibly against the current to get there. Surrender. And let the waves carry you back to your self.

II

SELF ESTEEM

"No matter how low you may have fallen in your own esteem, bear in mind that if you delve deeply into your self you will discover holiness there." – Thomas Merton

To Live In The World and Not In My Head

"Quiet is not a performance or a withholding; instead, it is an expressiveness that is not necessarily legible, at least not in a world that privileges public expressiveness. Neither is quiet about resistance. It is surrender, a giving into, a falling into self. The outer world cannot be avoided or ignored, but one does not only have to yield to its vagaries. One can be quiet." – Kevin Quashie, The Sovereignty of Quiet: Beyond Resistance in Black Culture (2012)

"For there is nothing either good or bad, but thinking makes it so." – Shakespeare

Great philosopher Britney Spears once said, "There's only two types of people in the world/The ones that entertain, and the ones that observe."[13]

Well, baby, I'm a put-on-a-show [in my head] kind of girl. In the world, I actually much rather prefer the back seat if I can help it.

85

My mind – I believe – is both my greatest asset and my most prolific enemy. I've always felt more connected to who I am to my self in my inner world.

The version of me that I am to my self, is open and her self and vulnerable and thoughtful. She's the star. She's who I wish I had the courage to be in the outer world. In the world, I don't feel like I show up in a way that displays confidence and security and self-belief.

It's not about escapism but about romanticizing, becoming attached to the promise of love and life. Adding magic and romance to an otherwise boring existence. I think that's why I love TV, film, art, and writing – pretty much all forms of storytelling.

My perception of what family dynamics were supposed to be like was modeled after sitcoms, of course. Full House, Family Matters, That's So Raven, Hannah Montana, etc. Whenever there was a family conflict on the show, there would always be the part at the end where after The Conflict™ the family would sit down and talk about the problem, find the moral of the story, hug it out, and the issue would be resolved.

I don't believe I grew up in spaces where that real, raw type of emotional honesty was a regular thing. I just don't think that was a thing in my family: Where we sat down and held space to flesh out our individual thoughts and emotions to and with each other.

I remember being alone to process and resolve a lot of

emotional complexity on my own. I believe I learned early on – specifically in my middle school years – that it was easier to figure out my emotional and mental issues on my own, especially as my emotions became bigger and more overwhelming. Not that the support was rejected, but when everyone around you seems endlessly preoccupied with other things, you learn after a while that it's just easier for everyone to try your best to figure out your stuff on your own.

I've always been a – not shy, but reserved person by nature. Combined with the fact that I simply didn't have the language to package my emotions "correctly" – I doubled down on this muted caricature of my self as I got older. So much so and to such an extent, that my intricacies as an individual human being in the world – my true thoughts, feelings, desires, opinions...essentially my identity – felt like they became flattened.

Especially when it all seemed "too much" or "too difficult." Looking back I know it was almost a form of escapism – a way to not have to deal with my big emotions or burden others with them either. It was easy to retreat to that space to avoid the reality of what I truly felt or thought at any given point in time.

I often felt like I couldn't undergo the process to discover my self by and for my self without the constant gaze of people who I felt already knew me and who I thought had a concrete picture of who I was and was becoming. It felt uncomfortable to just exist and experiment with different versions of my self that I wanted to try out in my adolescence.

I feel like it didn't allow me the breathing room (whether literally or figuratively) to fully stretch my self to fully explore who I wanted and liked to be in the world and with who I didn't want or like to be. I was always afraid of saying or doing the wrong thing, of being seen in a light where I wasn't yet fully self-assured (which at that time was every light from every angle). I was used to being the girl whose personality was quiet, reserved, and flat.

It was easier to accept not being seen and acknowledged at all than for people to do so only when you've made a mistake. That you would rather allow people to perceive you as such instead of correcting them. You, your existence, are not a mistake.

My inner world is wildly expansive – so much so that while there is room and potential for me to feel very full and content, the moments that don't feel achingly lackluster. And that, for me at least, feels worse than emptiness. But that is a very tall order for how life should feel.

There is a more reliable kind of hope that is born from deep loneliness. Having a gaze that is inherently fixated inward gifts you the ability to be curious about the broader world without being overwhelmed by it. I feel like you also need time in the quiet to find any thoughts, feelings, or words worth sharing, so it helps there, too.

But what happens when your life continues to move forward before you've found the words to capture your thoughts and feelings at that singular point in time? Before you've mustered up the courage to express all that has been sitting within you?

It leaves your nervous system feeling like a graveyard of unspoken grief and sadness, buried hopes and dreams. You end up becoming someone who places so much expectation on silence and stillness and in-between moments.

When you know the script, your marks – you can replay and reset and try again to perfect your performance. You can allow your body to go through the motions while your spirit grapples with whether or not it has true purpose in real life.

"If my blog were gone tomorrow..." – Blog Post, February 15, 2018

A few weeks ago, I had a moment of self-reflection and I asked my self, "If my blog were gone tomorrow, what would I have?" I mean (I think) I'd be okay if this little space on the Internet no longer existed. But as I kept thinking about it I realized that question echoed a similar tone of "Without my blog, what is my purpose?" Obviously, that sounds drastic and I know there's more to my life than this website, but this website and the opportunities, relationships, and experiences attached to it have undoubtedly defined my young adulthood thus far and I couldn't help but wonder what my life would be like without them.

When I started my blog my senior year of high school, I really just wanted to create a space where I could learn to better express my self verbally and creatively. I could never have predicted the people I have come to know because of this blog or the opportunities that this blog has created for me. Those of you who watch my Instagram stories know I'm always in my feelings about how God has blessed me when it comes to this specifically, but I genuinely mean every word every time. This blog means so much more to me than having my initials on a hat or rocking "yellow on some yellow like what purple is to Prince."[14] *This blog, and subsequently my brand, truly represents something that I've been able to put my whole heart into for the past two years that brings me genuine joy and excitement every day. This blog has created space for me at tables that I may not have otherwise had the courage or opportunity to ask for and the fact that people even recognize that tells me none of this was an accident.*

Going back to the original question, "If my blog were gone tomorrow, what would I have?" And I can confidently say if all of this were gone tomorrow, I would still have my voice. Regardless of this temporary digital space, I will always have my voice. I would still try my hardest to share my story so others feel inspired to do the same and I would still try my hardest to be an advocate for those who may not have a platform to make their own voice heard.

* * *

This started to shift in terms of how I showed up in the world when I first heard Audre Lorde's *A Litany for Survival* as well as the essay "The Transformation of Silence into Language and Action" which essentially talk about the imperative of speaking up even though – rather, especially when – you are afraid.

These works changed my life in terms of empowering me to

lean into taking up more space digitally through storytelling and in real life.

With the rise of social media, the internet became the place where I felt a little more comfortable with discovering my voice and sharing other aspects of my personality that I felt less comfortable displaying in real life.

It seemed easier to build a voice and platform online and to continue to lean into that voice and online platform because I didn't always feel seen and known in the way that I wanted to by the people around me.

But I quickly internalized that same gaze and hyper-self-consciousness that I had in real life. It felt more abstract and open to more energies than I could account for, let alone control.

Regardless, the version of me that I am and that I became to my self, is someone who knows how her story ends and is without fear.

She becomes addicted to that praise, allowing it to boost her ego enough to carry her to the next moment where she trades your doubt for her ephemeral initiative. Once the praise stops, she perceives those initiatives as ordinary and expected, the incentive to continue not as necessary. However, once the audience stops clapping or goes away altogether, forgetting all about its entertainer, she continues to do only what she's always known to do – perform – for she knows no other way of being.

This is how I feel most of the world operates: in a constant, never-ending performance. Individuals and institutions perform for those to whom they should be accountable. I wonder if we realize the extent to which we lie to our selves.

But what happens when the show ends? When the performance is over? Where do you go when you go quiet?[15]

What my messy room taught me about self-love.

This space was not set up for visitors. It never was.

You can try to rush to tidy up before they get there, but one day they will see the clothes spilling out of your closet door. Or, worse, they will show up unexpectedly before you've even had the chance to make the attempt.

In regards to rooms, or self-love, you must value your self enough to maintain a tidy, organized space regardless of if you will be the only one to occupy it. Under the assumption that you are going to be the only one to occupy this space, it is a reflection of your lack of self-regard to make your self live in a dirty room. By not regularly doing the laundry, leaving it in a dirty pile on the floor, and leaving it be because you're "the only one who has to deal with it" and only addressing the issue when you have company, further affirms to your self that you alone are not worthy of a clean room. Not doing the work to heal your wounds, address your unappealing qualities, or create the life you genuinely want to live until someone else presents the opportunity for you to do so, further illustrates to your self that you believe you are not worthy of having those things and getting them for your self. It illustrates a deep sense of self-hate, actually. Loving your self is more than a buzzword, a hashtag. It's more than face masks and wine and chocolate. It's consistently and unapologetically fighting for your past, present and future self. It's cleaning up your dirty laundry even though you're tired and had a long day at work. It's about buying the cute-but-overpriced decorations because even though you know you don't need them, they bring you a little bit of joy whenever you see them.

It's because you know that if someone decides to come crash at yours unexpectedly, you have a comfortable couch with extra blankets and pillows, maybe even an entire guest room, ready to go for them. Whether someone is there or not, you know you have made space for them and that it is tidy and comfortable, with no bearing on your life otherwise.

I fear creating things that other people might engage with. I don't think my purpose is to create a bunch of stuff for my self and my self alone (there's nothing wrong with that, I just don't think it's my calling). The other side of that, though, is constantly seeking approval and letting your audience be the authority of your art and expression. Of course, take constructive criticism, but don't get caught up in baseless hate or praise. I believe the fine balance is keeping my room (André 3000)[16] airtight and cultivating a space for me to truly perfect my craft, and then release it to the world when it's finished, and when I'm ready to open that part of my self to the world and give my audience that piece of my self.

I think the problem over the years is that I've had to share that room – that sacred space of critical thought, processing new information, synthesizing – with classes of over 20 other people. I don't believe I was ever given the space to understand how I learn and interact with information, which is really through on-the-job training, identifying information gaps as I go about my work and life, and interacting with the world. I live my life, observe, ask questions, and seek information. Having a foundation of knowledge to draw back on to make certain connections and have a basic level of understanding about most concepts is helpful.

Aloneness, clutter...it's easier to keep people out, rather than clean up reactively in response to other people's gaze – really their perceived criticism and judgment and misunderstanding. The goal was to move towards a place where I keep the room organized for my self, where my room provided space for comfort, care, rest and restoration, creativity, dreaming, and pleasure. That room is required for me to really get in my zone, but until I'm able to not be distracted by the fact that there's an audience perceiving me, I have a flow of being in my room, then being in the world when I'm ready to come out and I have a reason to be seen or heard. I'm not obligated to let people in my room, clearly, it's important to me for the sake of my relationships, so maybe the answer is boundaries, it's regularly taking time to my self to live life for my self and by my self, and reporting back the joy, experiences, revelations that I discover to those I care about. The point is to get something for me first.

* * *

A culture where material success is seen as paramount to personal and community development, can lead to low self-esteem in those areas and have devastating effects[17]. I think when interacting with my higher-ups and family, I sense that personal achievement is prioritized. With my peers and people closer in age, things like beauty, image, and clout seem to be more prioritized. In social situations with family or classes, I'm used to hanging in the background and "being seen, not heard" and find comfort when I can maintain that role in social settings, but when I'm expected to contribute to the conversation or in general maintain the same level of charisma as my peers, I find that I overthink and put pressure on my self to meet that cultural standard of extroversion rather than just be my self.

I'm very acutely aware of how people respond to me and notice when it's positive, negative, or indifferent. The latter two, I often take it personally due to my mother practicing under Toni Morrison's "Does your face light up [when you see children]?" I think that when I don't get that same enthusiastic response from people, or even indifference, I think that I did something wrong. I then try to overcompensate for whatever it is that I did to get the enthusiastic response.

I stopped caring about being accepted out of a deep fear that if I showed anything suggesting that I do, I wouldn't be accepted. The thought of "Do those I care about accept me for who I fully am and hope to become?" Doesn't even register because I've been so insulated in my own experience and trying to "figure it out."

Perfectionism = Give your self (or a project, task, assignment) the opportunity to just be what it is in this moment. Allow it to affirm itself in this present moment, and open up to be supported, helped, or taken to the next level.

Any artist or creative understands this idea: the conflicting actions of releasing your self into the world via your work but at the same time, hoping that no one will actually see you. The idea that by using our gifts to tell your story through art, a catchy song, or a piece of writing, no one will connect art to life or decode its seemingly metaphoric relationship.

What I realized from my journey into being a "content creator" (what I first heard folks call it once I got to Howard) was that I was actually using my blog as a means to avoid the difficult work of facing my emotions and the other human beings that triggered them.

I like to think of it as a persona or character who's looking for love and connection, who wants to be known and under-stood — not necessarily as an overwhelming or engulfing connection, but just knowing that you're cared for and that even if I desire freedom and agency and individuation and sovereignty I'm still known and loved and cared about, that I can trust that people will still hold me in the heart and mind with high regard.

My blog allowed me to take this one step further and mask my work as a way to help others by telling my story – which is still one of my primary motivators, but I was doing my self a disservice by not taking the time to properly unpack or consider my thoughts, emotions, and experiences and how they've shaped me into the person I am today, and continue to do so.

It was a great outlet for me to share my thoughts and ideas, and develop the voice that empowered me to write this book. That was good. But I realized it still wasn't enough. I still hadn't developed the tools and courage to truly reckon with my self, my thoughts, and my ideas as a person navigating the world in this body – to really be able to use my voice and be integrated into the world while using it. I was using my blog as a way to continue building up my internal world and narrative that felt like I was learning to be vulnerable and open and honest, but that was really keeping me insulated from the actual support and connection that I needed.

Notes – Love, Freedom, and Aloneness

> "Loving before watching: When you watch a thing before you love it (i.e. before you first decide to love it as it is), it becomes all too easy for that watchfulness to come from a place of hate and hyper-criticism. If you first decide to accept that thing as it is, before deciding to watch it, you have already decided that you will accept it even if it doesn't fit your rigid, idealized perspective." – Love, Freedom, and Aloneness (p. 19)[18]

I avoid making investments in my future, what shows

(to me at least) is that deep down I don't believe in my self or my future.

I do so under the guise of not knowing what the future will be and that I have no power in the unknown or in the world (because I cannot control it), which makes life – specifically the fact that I am becoming a real adult who has to take responsibility for her life – real.

I often project a hyper-critical perspective toward others because of the level of courage I wish I possessed. The thought of boldly putting my self out there at less than my best in a significant way is extremely scary. I get anxious at the thought of my worst fear being confirmed–that I am, in fact, not good enough—which causes me to freeze and move with extreme trepidation. Enough so to keep me on my proverbial bench, watching on as others live out their wildest dreams while I stay stagnant doing just that—dreaming.

It seems as though other people are not – like I am – stuck in apprehension but rather actively deciding, moving, and creating the life they want for themselves. The gap between dreaming and doing closes when I dare to act. When I refuse to allow my self to stay stuck in my inner world.

While it is safer here, while I have more control over my version of the world here, being stuck in my inner world does not do my self or the world any good. I would be remiss to withhold what God has placed within me in fear of not being in control of what's out there. My anxiety comes from the thought that whatever story I've told my self and believed was true may not actually be the truth. My anxiety comes at the thought that the real world is actually nothing that I thought it was, and that I'd actually have to take the time to get to know it for its truth instead of continuing to maintain a facade and sustain a perceived reality that is not rooted in the truth. That I'd have to sit with it and be vulnerable. Fully expose the worst parts of me and be fully exposed to the worst parts of it. And realize that, even after all that, we're stuck with each other—in sickness and in health, till death do us part. To know that since we're stuck together indefinitely, I better learn to love and accept it, and hope it will show me enough grace to do the same.

* * *

My first stint in therapy in 2018 taught me valuable lessons about learning to be vulnerable – like out loud, to other people. Namely, I got to experience what it felt like to be vulnerable in a space free from judgment, a space specifically held for me to talk about whatever was stressing me out without feeling like I was being dramatic. There was one time when that did happen, however, when I hesitated to share something because I thought I was tripping over it. But then I realized that I'm paying for it and that if I don't at least get it off my chest, it won't do anything but continue to wear away at me. So I shared it, and that was that. This led me to another revelation I had about vulnerability: Sometimes it is just a form of emotional and mental regulation. A way to clear out the gunk of residue in my mind left from the days or weeks before in exchange for an opportunity to live more mindfully.

My core perception of my childhood and life experiences up to this point is rooted in the belief that I didn't have anyone to open up to – more specifically, as I've come to realize, that I didn't trust anyone enough emotionally to open up and feel like I wouldn't be judged.

Whenever I did try to be vulnerable, I ~~never got~~ felt as though I didn't get the response that I wanted. I ~~never felt like they cared enough like they were being sympathetic enough, that they couldn't possibly understand what I was going through~~ didn't receive the empathy and compassion I needed and desired. Even if it was a totally acceptable response to my predicament, I would more often than not ~~take a mental note that I would not tell said person about my thoughts and emotions again and that, moving forward, I would try to figure it out my self~~ reinforce the same core beliefs about vulnerability and maintain stuck in an ego trap.

I've since learned that there is a distinction between expecting others to do my emotional labor for you, and needing the space to release and maybe even get an objective perspective on your situation if necessary. This distinction allows you to not only set emotional boundaries for your self and others, but it also allows you to take your self off the emotional training wheels you've been accustomed to wearing. This distinction clarifies your responsibility to do your personal work to understand your thoughts and emotions and take action (in real life) to change that which you cannot accept.

I believe that's why I love writing so much. I can divulge the entirety of my inner world on a page, using the best of the

English lexicon to make my darkest moments feel poetic, my most lost times reminiscent of the rising action of a play. I can easily edit and dramatize the telling of my own story and leave out my own culpable displays.

By doing this, I continue to occupy this fantasy world in which life is happening to me and that I am not, in fact, a major contributor to its unfolding. By using most of my time and energy to ponder my more difficult experiences as though I had nothing to do with them, did my higher self a disservice and only fortified my ego.

As a young adult, a lot of my work involves speaking up and making those unknown truths heard. I think that is important to get those unknown or unacknowledged, unarticulated truths out of your system to unlearn self-silencing (and understand why and under which circumstances I tend to self-silencing).

More importantly, I believe it's important to speak when you have something to say – when you feel convicted – when what you have to say is kind and uplifting, but also when it may seem uncomfortable, hard, or awkward. The only time I would advise not speaking is, of course, when what you have to say is harmful to your self or another, but specifically when it's just to fill a quota to say that you've spoken. Why do I always need to speak? Why does society force people into speaking? In corporate or academic settings, when you don't speak you become an imposition to a bottom line.

Our culture doesn't promote speaking to understand – it

promotes knowing everything and being sure and confident about everything, to have all the answers – which doesn't encourage people to speak up to be understood, to be curious, to say when they don't know but that they are open to learning. Our culture doesn't often promote listening, or the importance of honoring people's inner worlds, respecting that boundary of safety or comfort or trust. It doesn't promote speaking up even when the words don't flow out of one's mouth seamlessly but are rather imperfect and incomplete or inchoate. It doesn't promote the idea that in order to know, one has to start out not knowing, and that instead of being condescending and stingy with and about knowledge, we all have the opportunity instead to pass on information that is more and more correct with each iteration of speech – by correct I mean that it gets us closer to love, justice...truth. Information that gets us closer to the truth with each iteration of speech. And to pass on that information with love and care.

Inner worlds as sites of outer world-building

I discovered *The Sovereignty of Quiet* written by Kevin Quashie, on Twitter. It's a book that has broken my spirit open more times than I can count. To sum it up, it explores the concept of the Black person's inner world, compared to the better-known idea of Blackness as external, shared...loud.

"The sovereignty of quiet." I think about being a Black person, a Black woman, who is very reserved and soft-spoken, compared to the images and stereotypes we see of Black women in particular: We are supposed to be "loud and angry and ghetto."

I believe that in an effort to actively reject that notion, I also had trouble finding my self and staking my claim as an individual – one who didn't minimize her self because of cultural stereotypes, and who also didn't pretend to be who she knows she isn't because of how others might perceive her.

> "Quiet is not a performance or a withholding; instead, it is an expressiveness that is not necessarily legible, at least not in a world that privileges public expressiveness. Neither is quiet about resistance. It is surrender, a giving into, a falling into self. The outer world cannot be avoided or ignored, but one does not only have to yield to its vagaries. One can be quiet." – The Sovereignty of Quiet (pg. 45)[19]

It all goes back to gaze, and perspective, much of which for Black folks is informed and determined by whiteness, white supremacy, and white people. So much of who we are, what we do, and how we act is informed by how they see us and how they regulate our value.

* * *

I feel like being in the world and fully present in my body holds me down. When I'm in my head I can be and do everything everywhere at once.

I internalize that sitting idly by and being passive in life, would lead you to failure. That acting decisively was the only way to experience progress toward success until you're overextending your self and you don't know how to slow down because you feel like if you do, everything will inevitably crumble around you.

When you've grown up with so much stability and so much sameness, it's hard to recognize when the experiences and feelings you're clinging to are only still real in your head and no longer in reality.

That you've rested in the privilege of finding it easier to sit back and be a daydreamer – to reflect constantly about everything than it is to sit firmly and mindfully in one singular moment.

But there must be a balance of reflection and acting. A balance of knowing and thinking, and embodying.

> *"The real cause of this was pithily given by a Virginian tobacco planter: 'You can make a nigger work, but you cannot make him think.' No; education and a proper amount of self-interest alone can make a labourer (sic) a profitable and intelligent servant. In slavery, however, this is out of the question: a reflective slave is a dangerous 'article.' 'Negro property as it increases in intelligence decreases in security; as it becomes of greater value, and its security more important, more regard naturally paid to the means of suppressing its ambition and dwarfing*

its intellect.'

*Hence 'a well-informed capitalist and slave-holder'
remarked that – 'In working niggers, we must always
calculate that they will not labour at all except to avoid
punishment, and they will never do more than just
enough to save themselves from being punished, and
no amount of punishment will prevent their working
carelessly and indifferently. It always seems on the
plantation as if they took pains to break all the tools
and spoil all the cattle they possibly can, even when they
know they'll be directly punished for it.'" – Slavery and
Secession in America: Historical and Economical (pg.
215-216)*[20]

Trying to mask and somehow outwork my ADHD is what contributes to a lot of my burnout but it's not as easy as just not doing those things. Maybe because I struggle with feeling inherently worthy of the things I want and desire – the version of my self I hope to be and become. I feel like I have to work and earn and unhealthily strive toward those things – and that has caused resentment over time. I resent my self for the things about my self that I can't control and how that impacts my ability to move through life and be and receive what I want. I resent my self for not just being someone who is inherently deserving of goodness and good things.

I sometimes resent my self because I've over-internalized and personalized everything that the world tells me I am not. And I've over-indulged in the privilege of not having to fully engage actively in the world or my life and my identities that act as a liaison between the two.

I tried to feel – and if I couldn't…force – such a distinct separation between me and the bad, the unsure, the wrong of the world. To simply be in the world, but not of it.

And not in a self-righteous way, but in the way that I was subconsciously determined to shut my self out of the world and into my self, convinced that I was alone in like and experience. I did not want to accept that I am human and will and have inevitably felt those things and – by way of being socialized in this world, some of those things exist in me whether I acknowledge it or not.

I historically have been more willing to isolate my self completely to detach from uncomfortable situations than initiate the tough conversations needed to establish and maintain my emotional and energetic boundaries.

I knew that I couldn't get too lost or immersed in that internal world because I'd be naive and exposed/vulnerable/weak and susceptible to attack while not paying attention. That if I took a moment to stop being hypervigilant even when I needed to rest and regulate and give my self permission to simply be, everything would fall apart.

Journal – May 1, 2020

I spend so much time studying, reading, watching, and learning because I feel like no matter what I do, there's some part that I'm missing. The "secret sauce" to life that everyone has but me.

I think what it is that I fear is regret. I'm afraid that if I focus all of my energy on my self, I will run out of time, and miss fleeting opportunities. I am afraid that if I focus on my self, the world will move on without me and I will lose the opportunity to truly experience the world.

I feel like that is indicative of 1) an over-attachment to the world in general and 2) a false belief that my purpose will somehow actualize irrespective of the world at large. That tells me that I'm disconnected from the world, from my self and my emotions.

I think that I see a lot of what's going on in the world – the low vibrational, violent, evil, mean, and other negative energies in the world and think "Of course I don't relate to that." I believe that's an avoidance of the possibility that deep connection or integration with the world around you will reveal to you that you actually reflect some of those same qualities your self.

Or even more so, that there might be something in you that God is trying to pull out to influence those parts of the world, that you don't believe you have the power to. You believe that you have been tasked with saving the world all by your self and that is self-indulgent.

The world is so incredibly expansive (from what I've been told) and a life full of so many possibilities, but you think that your reason for existing in the midst of all of that expansiveness and possibility somehow does not involve other human beings and that you're all on your own individual, mutually exclusive journeys.

I'm a very loving and caring person towards people in general, but I think I haven't really been able to tap into that as far as my personal relationships in the way that I've wanted so I focus my energy on social justice issues because that's a way to show love for people and a way to show love for the people I care about by advocating for issues relevant to them.

I don't think it's about the politics (at least not stopping there), I believe it's more so about advocating for people's humanity and having that honored through our political system and social world at large. I have a hard time how translating that same level of love to the individuals in my life – I think it's about the same elements needed, knowing the person, their needs, dreams, and desires, and using your unique gifts and talents to try and make space for them to become their highest self while empowering them to self-actualize, heal and reach the fullness of their potential and commit to that journey themselves.

I have a very lofty imagination without the ability to be present and practice mindfulness with what is right in front of me. In that way, my imagination becomes more of a means of escapism instead of a potential tool to manifest a plethora of possibilities and develop a strong sense of faith and hope. I think the difference between the two is again, being present with the seemingly small things that are right in front of you, as they can help build your tolerance for the big things.

* * *

Demasking (overture)

I've always struggled with – not necessarily "being my self" in that I actively put on a persona that I perform in the world, but rather a version of my self that is much more held back, much more reserved, and, ultimately, much more flattened.

As you work on being more self-accepting, there is a moment when you start to realize…Everyone is pretending! Everyone is playing a character and living out a script that they have in their heads. And it's not one that we've written as an attempt to assert agency and self-determination in our own lives, but one that we've inherited from society, our families, and whomever else. Literally, everyone is pretending!

I've felt really strongly about this – to the point where it would almost make me upset that people "weren't being themselves" (as though that's something that I can determine for someone else). However, recently I asked my self – how much of that is a projection of the parts of me that wish I could move through the world as my character more confidently…or more that my character was a more confident or self-assured individual, to begin with.

It's almost like you're watching a TV show or movie (read: your life) and you think that a character is poorly written when in reality they might just be reflecting the parts of you

109

that you're ashamed of that you attempt to hide, rather than depict the qualities you wish you had. There's nothing for you to romanticize, nothing for you to lean into as a form of escapism. It's just you looking back at your self.

So, when I look at other people and think to my self – Is this person just pretending? Am I just interacting with their character and not them? I'm working to redirect that energy inward and ask my self – what qualities are they reflecting back to you that are making you feel this way?

It's an invitation to check in with my self to ensure I am showing up honestly and authentically, even when it may be uncomfortable to do so. I know I struggle with feeling safe to be and be seen as my completely authentic and open self. I now try to think: How can I create that sense of safety for my self so that I know I'm showing up honestly at all times, rather than waiting for someone to reflect that to me, and blaming my lack of openness in the interim on what I perceive to be their lack of openness?

At the end of the day, all of it is subjective and based on the stories we tell our selves and the script in our head that we are moving off of. That said, it's ultimately up to us to check in with our selves to ensure that our script is intentional and that it moves the plot forward in generative ways and brings us closer to authentic expression and connection.

What do I believe is at risk if I don't mask? What happens if I'm honest about the reality of who I am and what I have to work with in this life as a result of that – the good, bad, and indifferent?

Maybe I lose the potential to be held in high regard on whatever is left of the pedestal I feel like I have to salvage for love and belonging.

In that case, the delusions of grandeur – ambition and seeing your self as something or someone greater than the quiet daydreamer who feels stifled by identity, practicality, and responsibility – serve a bigger purpose.

I believe people create limited space or hold very rigid expectations of who they perceive me to be and what role they see me playing in their life, as opposed to creating a safe space for me to show up as my authentic self and then decide for themselves if that is good for their world.

After a while, you realize that you don't represent – or are not able to represent – these people, things, and places in a way that brings them glory and redemption. Sometimes it feels like I represent the things that people would rather keep in the background, but would still be useful to support their performance.

Your value is in your utility. And people rely on that utility. But they don't think you'll ever be exceptional. And because you have convinced your self to believe that your value lies only in your utility, you rely on it too.

For my self, I think the inability to be clear about who I am and what I bring to the table in my relationships and roles, then perpetuates my feeling that I have to perform in social situations, instead of giving my self permission to be my self and then acting accordingly.

My soul says to my self: I feel limited by this existence, having to navigate this world. In a linear, succinct way that makes sense for a consumer's gaze.

But when your ultimate desire is to experience meaningful connection, I feel like I'm not expressing my self fully/correctly/accurately – particularly when I can tell I'm not being understood. It almost triggers a feeling of failure: what are the obstacles that keep me from being easily understood and how can I work to remove them?

I'm thinking about this idea of having to play in your interactions with other people in different spaces and relationships. Having to play a different role for each of these people and in each of these spaces.

In these different roles and spaces and dynamics, there are different expectations or rules, unspoken rules, or needs that people in those spaces may be operating with and from.

Sometimes it feels clunky when everybody's operating from the space of what their needs are, how they're trying to show up in that moment, and their expectations for themselves and you.

Notes – April 20, 2023

Maybe there's something to be said about a power dynamic in terms of who initiates the pace, the tone, the kind of dominating structure maybe of what the expectations are around certain social rules and things like that...and how I think if you're not tuned in, locked into your self and intentional about who you are and how you show up in each moment or you're not secure in a very like foundational core identity, foundational core sense of self, or self-concept – I think that's where the overwhelm of like other people's expectations and these perceived expectations plays a role.

I overly identify with that part of my self – I am not that person, not because I don't believe I deserve it, but because that is the part I've always played in my life. That is the role I know.

I am overwhelmed and exhausted from the roles that I feel I have to play in everyone else's lives, by the role(s) that I am used to playing.

I don't believe I am acting in a way that honors my humanity. I move through the world as though I regard my own humanity as something that is to be observed and not participated in or self-directed.

I know that feeling is an innately human thing – but I am so limited by the fear that by expressing those emotions externally and by being witnessed in that expression, I expose my self to the risk of further isolation, abandonment, or invalidation.

It's a cycle of human emotions and expression – you think it just has to be the big things, at socially acceptable times and in socially acceptable spaces, so you can still control your emotions and how they're expressed.

I need a safe, controllable container to express my big feelings. But what about the tiny stressors that you say nothing about, the feelings and triggers you deem as small? Those pile up and become big, eventually. Be quicker to address those stressors early on, don't wait until shit is breaking down and you're still struggling to think "Okay now's the time I can maybe advocate for my self." Don't be like, "Oh I got it I got it." At least say something, don't pretend things don't bother you.

I know my social identities of course play a part in how I experience life and process those experiences – but it's all internal and rooted in how I experience(d) and connect(ed) with the world.

I've accepted that I always feel some level of disconnect within my inner world. I would like to think I live in a vacuum, where I can be free of those power dynamics and the extent to which I've internalized them – where I can just be.

I'm realizing that there seems to be power in trying to unlearn a victim mentality. To try and become someone who doesn't wait for the world to dictate her next move or give outside entities control over how she shows up, the one who actively chooses who and how she wants to be in the world. One who acts from that decision. from observing the phenomenon of life to actively participating in it.

I've spent so long settling for the dream, for the make-believe, that I don't think I understand what it would be like to experience the real thing: What it feels like to fully trust your self to show up in the world and navigate your life without needing to know all the answers and outcomes and predict and rehearse them. To execute the role of your self to perfection.

This past year, I started treatment for ADHD, and that has added another layer of urgency when it comes to taking up space, rather than just allowing my self to be someone who exists solely as an observer of life.

So my journey now is just about continuing to lean into moments when I feel like it would be easier to hide or stay silent, and instead make my voice heard and not shy away from how my identity as a young Black, neurodivergent woman impacts how I navigate the world.

I learned to use deliberate action as a catalyst for actualizing what I could imagine in my mind. As a tool to integrate my inner world with my physical reality. Sometimes the distance between the two seemed so far and like it would require much bigger leaps of faith. But I realize that I just had to look up and get out of my head to see how obviously close the next step was.

On Being Young, a Woman, and Colored

"So — being a woman — you can wait. You must sit quietly without a chip. Not sodden — and weighted as if your feet were cast in the iron of your soul. Not wasting strength in enervating gestures as if two hundred years of bonds and whips had really tricked you into nervous uncertainty.

But quiet; quiet. Like Buddha — who brown like I am — sat entirely at ease, entirely sure of himself; motionless and knowing, a thousand years before the white man knew there was so very much difference between feet and hands.

Motionless on the outside. But inside? Silent."
– Marita Bonner, *On Being Young–a Woman–and Colored* (1925)[21]

"There is no such thing as a single-issue struggle because we do not lead single-issue lives." – *Audre Lorde*, Learning from the 60s (1982)[22]

116

A lot of things that I can't change about the world are reflected in my self and in those around me – a definition of my self that I cannot control.

I feel a chasm between the vision I have for my self and my life and the reality of what it means to be this soul navigating this world in this body. A chasm that breeds resentment for the journey my soul has me on in this lifetime.

Maybe I feel burdened by my own corporeality. There's a feeling of wanting to separate my self from social identities and labels to escape the "noise" and figure out who I truly am at my core – my essence, spirit and soul.

At the same time, I understand how that essence manifests as and is informed by my social identities (and vice versa, how my essence informs my social identities).

Social norms and gender constructs feel rigid and superimposed, teaching young Black girls to be weak and complicit, to play a background role in "a white man's world."

And as much as I want to believe I can defy that burden, the world very quickly and very frequently reminds me that's just not the case. It slows me down and forces me to deal with my own and society's bullshit.

Blackness, womanhood, and youth feel like having to accept subjugation to power that is not and can never be mine. The denial of resources and privileges that I do not and will never have access to. And it's often juxtaposed or justified with valiant acts of Black female superheroism, magic, and other illustrations of how we have been forced to defy the odds in every aspect of life.

I imagine my self lying on the floor, with the other walking up to me – I don't know whether they're planning to curb-stomp me out, or lay an offering at my side. They could just be walking by with no intention of acknowledging me at all, or staying for long.

The point is the lack of control, the fear, the powerlessness. It's feeling highly visible and invisible at the same time.

It's like my soul is saying, I feel trapped in this person – their identities, their story. Outside of all of these identities, I come back to my inner world for agency and peace and…well, quiet:

> *"Central to existentialism is a consideration not only of power but also of agency–how the force of the world manifests against the will of the individual, and what the nature and meaningfulness of action are in the fact of such force. These questions are also important to the notion of quiet, though they might be phrased in a slightly different way: how to live life fully without being trapped by the expectation of resistance, how to engage the agency of the inner life?"* – The Sovereignty of Quiet *(pg. 55)*

I don't speak on behalf of Black women or the Black community, but obviously, in terms of identifying as young and Black and a woman, all bring on their own respective challenges – imagine finding your self at the intersection of all three.

The point is not to abandon all of these identities or the person they have brought me to be. Again, it's to recognize and honor the purpose they serve(d).

* * *

As I've grown and matured – and by grown and matured I mean as I've accepted the reality of the world I live in – it's a sweet idea to think that I can shield my self from violence in this world by dressing "modestly" and wearing my hair "professionally." By not speaking too loudly or out of turn and by instead being meek and overly agreeable.

I always just kind of went along with what people told me to do – I was a people-pleaser, but even more so I just minimized my self so as to not cause problems. While I was successful in that, not causing (too many) problems. I internalized this automatic response of making my self small. I learned that being seen for the sake of being known is not the same as being seen for the sake of being desired or consumed.

It's how many Black people are socialized to survive. It's how women and girls are socialized to avoid violation. It's how young children learn to survive to prevent being abandoned by their caregivers and the adults in their lives.

Learning these rules and staying inside the preconceived lines was not an instinct for pick-me-ism, but rather for survival –

119

more socially and emotionally than physically.

As a young person – if I follow the rules and am obedient in formal educational institutions, I convince my self that will keep me safe. As a woman – if I follow the rules and am compliant while navigating a world driven by patriarchal violence, I convince my self that will keep me safe. As a Black person – if I follow the rules and am compliant, I convince my self that will keep me safe from white supremacist violence.

This response, however, is ultimately driven by a very innate human fear of suffering, which happens to have manifested itself through the simultaneous conditions of my being young, a woman, and Black. These three intersecting identities put me in a position to fear the world and society and individual people, yet still have to depend on them for my own survival and to meet my needs.

So much of being young, a woman, and Black – for me – feels like constantly being denied the things that you most desire – or rather accepting an identity in which you believe those desires will inevitably be denied or taken from you. Maybe the first thing being my self.[23]

It feels like constantly being attuned to the fear of imminent violation. The inevitable subjugation and restriction of your personal agency. And it feels like that reality has rendered my self-concept flat, and any opportunity of experiencing deep, sincere freedom, joy, connection, or community, obsolete.

I feel the actually very abstract fear of experiencing suffering and harm to my psyche and physical body, which is then personified through narratives of women experiencing sexual and interpersonal violence at the hands of their male partners, young Black children and teens being murdered in the streets by police or young children having their autonomy – and, ultimately, their spirits – stripped down by (at its best) educational spaces that prioritize subordination and (at its worst) function as a de facto carbon copy of carceral institutions.

When all of that is imprinted on one's psyche, the response, for me at least, has been to narrow your self down so much as to erase all of the qualities that are brought to life through those intersecting identities. Yet that is still not enough.

Do You Really Want To Live Forever Young?

When you're a kid you're supposed to be immortal[24]. Ideally in the literal sense, but more so in the sense that when you're a kid you're supposed to have limitless energy for limitless dreams and the limitless potential that you imagine for your self. When you're older you recognize that not only are you literally mortal but that you only have energy and time and space to embody one life, so you must consolidate all the versions of your self that you believe you can be into one body.

There is a certain kind of grief inherent to the transition from childhood and adolescence to young adulthood. In your childhood, you have the freedom, joy, and lightness of unlimited potential. I've learned that as I've gotten older (albeit I'm very much still in my youth), with every life transition and major decision, that limitless potential seems to dwindle little by little.

With each decision – from what college I wanted to go to, the job I want to have postgrad, to where I'll live in my first official apartment by my self (or back home with my parents) sets me up for the next thing. With each decision, I'm building my one, singular life. And I'm aware of the fear that one day, there won't be any more decisions to make. My life will have been lived and there will be nowhere left to go.

That sounds awfully dramatic, and some might say I should instead revel in my youth and in the opportunities that I have ahead of me. With that, I've realized another kind of fear that I've been avoiding – of what it means to be actively aware of and involved in your life. I used to see adults when I was a kid and dream of the day I got older because that's when I'd be free to do my own thing. I'd have the room to just *be*. But the relief of finally having that room to be is only half the battle of *being and becoming*.

It's barely scratching the surface of realizing all the small, but important decisions that make up a daily life over the course of a lifetime. It's being hyperaware of all the small decisions that could lead you down multiple different paths. It's a constant anxiety about those decisions as you make them because then you realize that this is it. This is living. And I don't think I was prepared for that as a kid. How to cope with the reality of living.

But my introduction to what it meant to be a Black kid, a Black girl, in America was by learning about the 16th Street Baptist Church bombing – specifically through watching HBO's *4 Little Girls* documentary. It illustrated to me what it meant to navigate a world where such violence toward children was even conceivable, but I don't think I was in the position to really understand and grapple with that. With the reality of dying.

I feel very strongly about how the world treats Black children, and how they are made to feel like burdens for simply taking up space in the world. As a young Black girl, you internalize all of society's burdens in the form of behavioral correction and patronization.

When you have the privilege of being a Black child who is (or feels) a little more sheltered physically, you instead learn quickly that it's easier – safer – to just go along with what other people say and tell me to do – specifically adults. And white folks. Anyone in a position of authority and power over you, which as a little Black girl, feels like everyone.

It's not even that I desire to instead be someone who thrives on being bossy (or the boss), or correcting people when they're wrong – but as a young adult, I struggle to offer a new way of thinking, being, or doing and feel confident that others will be open and receptive to that.

I internalized a fear of correcting people or presenting an opposing perspective so as to not cause that – or any – discord. If I felt like someone was wrong, I'd just do whatever they said, or smiled and nodded, and go and do my own thing behind the scenes.

Some people perceive me as a goodie-two-shoes rule follower, but it actually is different than that. I find that I don't gel well with people in positions of authority, but I also don't want to deal with (read: fear) the repercussions of not following the rules, because in my experience, people in positions of authority like to make a show out of punishing you and letting you know you're wrong.

It doesn't create psychological safety that we need to feel comfortable sharing the thoughts, opinions, and feelings that make us who we are. It doesn't give children or youth (or even other adults) insight into the bigger picture goal, shared values, and the understanding that we're interconnected and should learn how to better work together. It places an unwarranted precedence on the feelings, opinions, and judgments of those in positions of power, and even more so, invalidates the feelings, opinions, and judgments of those who are not in positions of power. In schools, families, society overall...the latter people who experience this the most are almost always children.

As an adult, I now understand that people want to feel heard and like their perspective or approach is valued. I always thought that I grew up around a bunch of people who cared about being right and asserting their rightness, more than they cared to provide a genuinely safe space for me. In professional spaces, and generally, in different spaces in life, I still feel the subtle ways the world attempts to patronize and infantilize

Black people, Black women, and young adults in general.

I also now understand as an adult how learning to share your ideas, assert boundaries and advocate for your self, or ask for help are all things that we often – even in small ways – deny children the opportunity to do. And if we do allow them the opportunity, we often minimize or disregard them altogether. And rarely do we ever make the connection between the adults we are today and the children we were.

Not a girl, not yet a woman

As a young, Black woman – I cannot be weak because weakness gets you exploited. Conversely, I internalized stereotypes of Black women – much of which directly pertain to our emotions and how they present or how we express them. I was extremely self-conscious about being perceived as a loud and/or angry Black girl.

I do not want and have never wanted to passively accept the patriarchal directive to play small, conform, and embody subjugation[25]. Certain brands of feminism make it seem as though the only way a woman can assert their power is loudly and fiercely. My nature is and has always been to be more quiet and reflective – it gives me space to explore my agency and how and what I think and feel, and how I express what I think and feel. I get frustrated when I'm in interactions where I think that is perceived as weakness, where weakness is expected, as opposed to genuine support for your individuality and personhood. Because there is either

125

internally fulfilled agency and externally assumed complicity, or performative agency that is still for an external audience.

As a young, Black woman – "not knowing" is not an option. It feels like other women (white women and non-Black women of color) have more room to be dainty, ditzy, and clueless.

I think about how fun it must be to wear pink pussy hats and nasty woman shirts. To not have to worry about dying during childbirth because of implicit racial bias at the hands of a doctor. Or being a young Black girl and criminalized or brutalized by a school resource officer because someone thought you had an attitude. Or being a Black trans woman and simply trying to survive.

To fight for gender parity without feeling obliged to acknowledge all the ways in which Black women are still left behind.

I have always hated how people who do not know me, and who have not worked to get to know me – my experiences, wants, needs, thoughts, and feelings – are in positions to make influential decisions with powerful implications and consequences for my life.

Maybe even more so: that even though I felt the desire to assert and declare my own agency, I resent my self in moments when I don't know my wants, needs, thoughts, and feelings. Within and for my self, let alone to shield my self from the world and everyone in my small corner of it trying to tell me who I am – what I want, need, think, and feel.

I sit deeply in the struggle between inner limitlessness and a complete lack of social power as a young Black woman.

As a young, Black woman – I fear being consumed by others' needs, but I also fear not being needed at all, of being invisibilized and forgotten about. Being needed feels limiting and in conflict with my desire for autonomy.

There is a lot of messaging on who to not be – lazy, angry, over-emotional, naive, clueless, "green," disagreeable, unpleasant, needy, etc. – because you won't be an undue burden to other people around you.

In the eyes of some, if you don't willingly participate in your own objectification that makes you less of a woman, but, in the eyes of others, if you do willingly participate in your own objectification that makes you less of a woman worthy of respect.

I discredit my self very often because I believe I have to be perfect – that I have to have all my T's crossed and I's dotted before I think about taking a step. This does nothing but waste time and gives more space to those who are, quite frankly, a lot more mediocre and a hell of a lot more bold in their mediocrity.

This world teaches young girls to strive to be seen for the latter. It teaches young girls that our value is equivalent to *if* we are seen, rather than *how* we are seen – and even more so, *who* is seeing.

Society unequivocally teaches girls and women to value the patriarchal gaze more than it teaches us how to bring our awareness to our perception of our selves, and how to judge if our behaviors are in alignment with the person we want to become.

Even through a lens of mainstream white feminism: its entire perspective is rooted in trying to become equivalent to men, only to affirm the very false idea that they are the standard in the first place. When it comes to educational opportunities, wages, housing, medical care, respect, support, and being heard in our interpersonal relationships and respective communities – the gauge shouldn't be "Are we getting the same amount as men?" but rather "Let's focus on what our needs are, and ask for more until we feel satisfied with that."

But, within a patriarchal society, and especially in a society where #GirlBoss feminists exist, even that conversation will still be centered around furthering the privilege of those who benefit from whiteness, certain countries and classes of origin, being able-bodied, and/or cisheteronormativity, and their attempts to get more than enough, while everyone else struggles for just enough.

Education As a Site of Liberation

My education probably had the biggest influence on my self-esteem and belief in my self-efficacy. My understanding of power dynamics and my social positioning in the world.

One thing I see a lot on social media discourse and elsewhere (read: real-life discourse) is how we should learn about finances – credit and mortgages and insurance – in school. How other life lessons should come from our teachers within the four walls of an educational institution.

I don't disagree with most of that, but I think back to my own childhood and my teachers and think – I don't really want to learn about life from these people. There's a certain disconnect I experienced because of where I grew up, in a predominantly white town, with only a few Black teachers – only one of whom was a Black woman, and a multitude of people with decision-making power and influence over my life who couldn't speak to anything about my experience in the world as a Black girl.

My experience with my education was that I was just passively being given information, with no consideration of how I learned or what I wanted to learn. When certain things didn't work or make sense for me, I didn't feel empowered to say that or really seek support, because I thought I had it better than other students who might have been really struggling for whatever reason, so I didn't want to take up that space and resources from someone who actually needed it.

Layers of power dynamics that I realized in school – always striving to this place of being older and wiser, assuming that it just automatically comes. But are you actively seeking out knowledge, new information, and experiences, reflecting on and questioning the root source of your beliefs and way of thinking and being? That's how you become wise.

Adults in my life didn't often create opportunities for me to learn critical thinking. You either knew or you didn't. But education is meant to serve as the connection between those who know and those who don't, older generations and younger. Those categories don't overlap in a black-and-white way. I wasn't really empowered by the experiences I *did* have and the things I *did* know as a kid. My voice and my perspective weren't always affirmed, even if it was wrong.

There's a lot to be said about how that shows up in educational spaces, our families, and our interactions with the justice system – but overall, we're taught to blindly follow those in positions of power rather than exercise creative noncompliance. I learned that word recently from the High Tech High Graduate School of Education and was really empowered by it because it spoke to a concept that I needed to learn and be encouraged to practice as a kid. To have the critical thinking and judgment skills to understand what people are asking me to do and why. Adults never had a why. It was just because "I said so."

> "As an alternative, Freire proposes 'problem-posing' education as an alternative to banking education. Under problem-posing, the teacher would teach as well as learn from the student. This way, the student has a more active role in her educational experience. The ability to ask questions and to come up with their own theories is the basis of the students' role in problem-posing. This is similar to what 'progressive' education strives to emulate in the classroom.

130

> *John Dewey probably would have looked at problem-posing as an accommodating substitute for traditional education. Both Freire and Dewey saw traditional education as too restrictive and mechanical, however, Dewey also expressed his concern with an education that seeks to maximize 'freedom.' Whereas Freire states that education should provide a path to freedom, Dewey argues that education should be based off of experiences and encourage a lifelong path to gaining knowledge and wisdom through the accumulation of beneficial experiences." – Freire on Freedom of Education*[26]

There is a common saying that goes, "Be the person you needed when you were younger." I needed someone to be frank with me, to let me know when I was wrong, but to do so gently, in a way that corrected my missteps without leading me to believe I was a bad person or incapable of doing right. I see how people speak to their children. I see how teachers treat children. That they need to get in line because there are "things to do."

The point is confidence. Society doesn't offer space and grace for Black children to develop healthy confidence.

To Be Young, Gifted, and Black

I hate the saying that's popular among Black kids from the suburbs or other predominantly white communities – "Too white for the Black kids and too Black for the white kids."

When I actually unpack that and ground that in the reality of my experience – I think about class, my relationship to money as it pertains to social status and participation, how that leads you to believe you have to perform for white folks in all facets of life to get by, particularly in educational and career spaces.

I feel like white people (or non-Black folks) only see a Black person, and that they are interacting with me out of the assumption and expectation that I will perform to that. More often than not, they see and project the stereotypes they've been fed about Black people.

There's a part of me that wants to say it made it easier to be my self – in some Black spaces, and maybe this is more to do with my being neurodivergent, I was always afraid of being perceived as sensitive, nerdy, and weird.

I have always cared more about – placed more precedence, or have always been more attuned to – how other Black people perceived me than about how I was perceived by white folks. I know they *see* me – for better or for worse.

I know that I have always been rooted in my Blackness, I just didn't have places back home to really reach out and connect with something that looked and felt familiar.

When I got to Howard it became clear that...yes, everyone here (for all intents and purposes) is Black. So who are *you*? What else do you have to offer besides being Black? What do *you* have to offer to this space and this community? And how will you stand confidently in that offering?

I pray that growing up where I did, and then going to an HBCU, prioritizing being in Black spaces, continues to show me how my personality and existence can go beyond my Blackness. I am absolutely grounded in the fact that my experience is 100% enriched by my Blackness and by getting to interact with and experience more diverse forms of Blackness, but I also am learning that I, as an individual, have so much more to offer to the world beyond that.

And no shade, no beef – but you can tell when someone's whole personality and origin story revolves around the fact that they were the only Black person in the room. When that is the foundation from which they build their self-concept.

For me, my Howard experience dismantled this perspective to show me that Black people, the Black diaspora, and the Black experience are all inherently multifaceted. The issue is and was the media, and how I over-internalized that – the media's portrayal of Black folks – as truth and dismissed what I saw, felt, and experienced in my actual day-to-day life.

Instead, I saw my personal reality as an anomaly that was not reflective of the real world, which contributed to the feeling that the world was going to catch me off guard for a rude awakening – a feeling of "waiting for the other shoe to drop."

I internalized the idea that navigating the world as a Black person and a woman meant constantly being on guard because your body could be harmed at any moment.

While that is disproportionately true for Black people and women, I had to be honest about the fact that I haven't experienced the worst of it and didn't really saw things like that happen in my hometown – less because of actual safety and absence of white supremacist and patriarchal violence entirely, but more because I was very sheltered from a lot of those issues and experiences. However, it instilled a fear of being out in the world freely because I could still potentially be putting my self in harm's way. It wasn't an outwardly anxious fear, but a silent withdrawal from the world. I later learned language for this – vicarious racial trauma.

And so now, when I'm doing sociopolitical work and work in community. I feel a level of disconnect, I realize that I have found comfort in isolating my self to be able to help Black people from a distance, without being intimately in community, bound up in one another's struggle. I try to just throw my self back into those spaces without realizing that the root problem was never addressed. That said – how do I find security in my self to connect and be in community with others?

I've tried on a personal level to shift my perspective, heal and improve my own biases, but there are still a lot of systemic inequities that prevent the vast majority of people, particularly our society's most vulnerable, from achieving self-actualization.

What good is it to "find your self" and not be able to actualize that self to the fullest potential? "Life, liberty, and the pursuit of happiness" and the "American Dream." So many obstacles in place that prevent people from achieving that. An ideal society, I believe, is one in which people are institutionally and communally supported in becoming who they were put on Earth to be. But even then, is that a valid expectation – or rather, is it even a priority?

Should it even have to be said that as human beings, we should be able to rely on the social institutions and networks we have to support us in our growth? Given the way that we have historically chosen to organize our selves as human beings – in and under the institutions of family, marriage, church, education, government, and economy – we all participate in unspoken agreements that maintain and uphold these institutions. Most of which do not actually offer that hope and promise to our society's most vulnerable.

The definition of a social institution acknowledges that they are structured on values, which in America's case are the values of white supremacist patriarchy and capitalism. At what level do we balance tradition (what we know and what is baked into our ways of being) with, at the bare minimum, progress and reform – and ideally, abolition and transformation?

While reforms, like *Brown v. Board* in the case of education for example, have allowed for some progress, the fundamental paradigms that inform biases about what (academic) excellence looks like, and how students should arrive at that point disproportionately affect Black students and shapes their beliefs about their capabilities and ability to self-actualize in this life.

I believe my feelings about the educational institution at large are because that was twelve-plus of the most formative years of my life that I'm not getting back. It's more than one bad teacher or a few bad grades. It's me now realizing the major parts of my internal work and healing are rooted in my educational experience and the limiting beliefs it instilled in me about my self and the world and my potential in it.

I will always be an advocate for educational equity, and more importantly for children, for the cause of listening to and validating children – their voices and experiences – because there is a lot of messaging they pick up that we think they are oblivious to that actually sticks with them subconsciously. We invalidate our children and make them feel like their voices and agency don't matter and wonder why we deal with a lack of personal conviction and confidence as adults.

Particularly for Black people, we are often taught to place our worth in our proximity to white spaces, only to get in them and be disregarded and unsupported.

We adopt that mindset, erasing the complexities of each of our individual personalities and humanity in exchange for a shared identity – Blackness – only to be juxtaposed with whiteness. Obviously, as a form of survival, to hopefully bring some solace and relief in the idea there is another like me who sees and understands me. However, we inadvertently – or advertently – do so much damage to one another when we try to erase the complexities within another that we don't give our selves permission to access and embody, particularly in the attempt to acquire more proximity to whiteness.

136

Sometimes the Black experience can be so homogenized that we forget that we are human beings with souls that are navigating our own unique expression of that in this lifetime. Kevin Quashie explores this as well in *The Sovereignty of Quiet* – the idea of Black folks' uncritical solidarity based on our race.

> *"The narrator notices a distinction between a community of people whose relationship is 'unperturbed' and 'calm' and shaped by their shared beliefs; and a community 'flung' together on the basis of nothing but color. The sarcastic tag, 'Unless color is, after all, the real bond,' accentuates the point that she has made—that color alone is not sufficient to determine humanity or kinship; certainly, color does not equate to desire and ambition and interior subjectivity."* – The Sovereignty of Quiet *(pg. 32)*

When I am honest about the patterns of community I experienced among Black people, I realize that I maybe subconsciously just knew I needed to flock to be near Black folks because I knew white and non-Black people were definitely not safe.

I realized that the relationships I formed solely based on shared racial identity were sometimes actually really empty. There was the internal assumption – or the hope – that being around a group of Black people would offer me automatic safety. But on further recollection, there were definitely instances where it did not guarantee or even attempt to promise me psychological or physical safety as a child or adolescent, as a woman, or as a neurodivergent person.

I haven't always felt entirely safe or accepted or seen with care and compassion by other Black people – by other Black girls, especially by Black boys and now men, often by older Black women. That is my reality – although I understand now the internal things others may have been carrying might've led to that.

Nevertheless: What does actual safety in connection and community mean for me? Solely focusing on Blackness erases the fact that I am a unique individual with needs and wants that, while not necessarily new under the Sun, are specific to me and my life.

Nobody Likes You...When You're 23

When you're young you're more shortsighted.

But, when there's an expectation of and constant fixation on your future you become super long-sided, almost to a fault. So much so that you forget to or never learn to be present with and hold space for your present-day self.

Or, there's almost an assumption of short-sightedness – to the point of recklessness. That you shouldn't be thinking about the future, even though you have high hopes for a good or even great life, and you want to be sure that you're being intentional about how you get there and whether or not you're on the right track.

I internalized as a child that needing support or not knowing what I ought to know was inconvenient to others...that I was inconvenient to others. So I adopted a mentality of needing to figure everything out my self as to not place an added burden onto the adults around me – who I could visibly and energetically tell were stressed or overwhelmed themselves.

As an adult, who is now often stressed and overwhelmed by the responsibility of adulthood, I have maintained that same mentality of needing to figure things out my self instead of seeking support and leaning on my support system – cultivating a support system – even if just emotionally to vent and decompress.

I know I am capable of doing things on my own, but I guess just not all at once.

I think it's more the mental stress of the pressure that causes you to ensure you're getting to everything. I think when adults are burdened and unsupported, inadequately cared for, that affects children no matter how you slice it or try to hide it or try to compartmentalize it. They absorb and feel that. It creates a cycle of people not being in a position to support and show up for others because we our selves are not supported. And it's so easy for children to bear the burden of being viewed, and more importantly treated, as yet another inconvenience rather than an impressionable human being who simply didn't ask to be here.

We get short with children, we disconnect emotionally and mentally from where they are – where we were at their age. We don't understand why they don't understand. We project our frustrations onto them because it's easy. We don't direct that energy onto the systems and circumstances that create difficulties for them, or that create difficulties for us and prevent us from being able to show up for them and support them adequately. Because that feels harder and more insurmountable. But children don't see that. They see that when they mess up or don't understand something, they make people angry or frustrated. They don't see the surrounding circumstances, they internalize that as a perception of themselves.

When I see this happen to little Black girls now, I can't help but see my self. Whenever they make a mistake or reach a difficult fork in the road, they get frustrated. They give up. They don't gear up to bat again because they don't believe they can. They approach the first try with confidence but when they are knocked down once – God forbid twice – that confidence visibly leaves their spirit and takes any semblance of hope with it.

When these little Black girls are reprimanded for being too much when they are simply being themselves, they feel othered. They feel as though they are not and will never be accepted for who they are.

When I see this happen to little Black girls, I trace back the steps to when I first began to lose my self. I see the origin of the young Black woman in her 20s, who has a deep inner knowing of the woman she wants to be but can't shake the voices of everyone who made her feel like she can't or shouldn't – mainly because she's adopted it as her own inner voice.

I didn't need anyone to hold my hand every step of the way, to coddle me, or to make excuses for me. What I needed as a child was compassion and grace. I instead internalized the belief that I couldn't do anything right and would be discarded or forgotten because of it. People see me as the young adult I am today – this person who struggles to feel confident and feel like she'll be seen fully in her identity outside of her achievements – and forget that.

The girl I see in the mirror today bottles up her emotions like it's second nature, she doesn't fully understand the purpose or process of asking others for help, she feels stuck cosplaying the Superwoman Complex because she still believes that in order to ensure that she is remembered and cared for at the end of the day she must simply do it her self.

And because others expect it but didn't always explicitly demand it from her, because that's just who she is and has become, she internalizes that someone somewhere will always be peering over her shoulder, expecting her very best 100% of the time. She internalizes it to the point of overexerting her self (or feeling like she has to) in order to appease those around her.

What she doesn't realize is that most of this is not of her own volition. She believes it's her own expectations of her self and her life when really it is a subconscious attempt to prove to everyone around her – namely her self – that she is, in fact, important and special and worthy of being seen and valued, and remembered.

* * *

I have learned that what I believe I struggle with is relational self-esteem, or confidence in my belonging, because when the world reflects back to you that you don't matter, what you know to be true about your self or your potential doesn't matter so you don't trust that inner knowing. You know you inevitably have to accept how others perceive you and defer to the implications of how others perceive you on your life's outcomes.

The actual message was that women, children, and Black people were assumed or expected to be passive or lazy or useless – God forbid you throw being neurodivergent in there.

My response to this was to believe that I had to be larger than life and to do all the things to surpass those assumptions and expectations. I became hypervigilant about my desire to be and feel seen and understood, which at times led to an overreaction in moments when I feel misunderstood: "If they just better understood me, where I was coming from, why do the things I do – the outcome could be different."

My pervasive anxiety about needing to prove my value and my worth is what keeps me stuck in the past. But is there any other way to resolve it and find peace other than "letting it go," which just feels like a repackaged version of invalidation? Maybe I have a hard time accepting and letting go because I am still afraid that by doing so I'm admitting weakness or fallibility or lack of control.

To know that there is so much in you but to feel so limited in your ability to actualize it. Thinking that I'm playing against the limiting expectations that the world has of Black women, children, and people with ADHD, when really at some point it just became me against my self without me realizing it.

My inner world feels like it is all that I have: The world tells me every day that I don't have my body, and what I do with that body has to be in service to or performance for racial capitalism and patriarchy.

It tells you actually aren't good enough or worth anything – which might justify feeling disregarded or outright disrespected.

The world teaches you that you should hate your self before you even have a solid foundation of who you are.

It teaches you that there's not space for you – and a space that is there is intended to exploit you.

And when it teaches and requires you to not see, offer compassion and empathy to your self, how could you possibly offer that to others?

I want to be seen and cared for as a human being – not praised for how efficient and how disconnected I am or was from my own wants and needs. But I'm afraid that if that were to happen, it would inherently transform the nature of my relationships – with and to my self, my work, and other people. My dreams and aspirations.

I think it would transform them because I would no longer be able to uncritically participate in them or chase them with the same desperation. But I struggle with how to reconcile that and still move forward with choosing what is best for me in my life and who I want to be in it

Questions about gender and race have invited me to think deeper and are things that I've thought about, but it's literally as simple as rigid gender norms stripping me of my perceived access to agency and ability to explore and to find my self for my self. To discover and actualize what I believe is possible for my life as a result of what I decide I want and envision.

There's a certain ease of being that comes from just allowing all parts of you to simply exist, and being able to decide how and to what extent that shows up in any particular moment

I'm moving beyond just seeing my self as other's projections and definitions – social identity as a young Black woman or as a shy/quiet/weak person — and to actually knowing my self and understanding what I want my unique expression to be in the world.

However, I still don't believe that discovering your self is about deciding and projecting that, it's just getting to better understand your self. It really doesn't have anything to do with anyone else, it's an intimate journey that I need the space to take on, without all of the external noise, to be honest with my self about the way that I have internalized those projections and allowed them to limit my perception of my potential[27] and contort my self-concept into something I don't know I actually want it to be.

Don't Be a Lady, Be a Legend

"This is a story about control
  My control
  Control of what I say
  Control of what I do
  And this time, I'm gonna do it my way (My way)
  I hope you enjoy this as much as I do
  Are we ready?
  I am
  'Cause it's all about control (Control)
  And I've got lots of it" – Janet Jackson, Control (1986)

"In order for the return to the positive to be genuine it must involve negativity, it must not conceal the antinomies between means and end, present, and future; they must be lived in a permanent tension; one must retreat from neither the outrage of violence nor deny it, or, which amounts to the same thing, assume it lightly."
– Simone de Beuviour, The Ethics of Ambiguity (1947)

I've always been intrigued by women's anti-hero roles, not when they characterize and further stereotype them as evil villains (read: mean women), but because they give permission for young girls to not adopt a mandate of being overly nice and perfect. Where niceness as performance is not expected, but kindness, respect, and benevolence are a choice, where it's a treatment that has to be earned from another and not demanded or, again, expected – especially from Black women.

For me – it was Gabrielle Union's Julia in *Daddy's Little Girls.* She was the career-driven, super successful lawyer who took no shit from men – enough so that she seemed like the archetypal career woman who couldn't get nor keep a man.[28]

I didn't want to be her but, at some point, I found my self on that path to becoming her – because it was just easier to put my energy into a career, to double down and focus when things get uncomfortable or difficult, easier than situations where the only path forward is to be vulnerable and open my self up to care and support and love.

The pushback I witnessed happening against these women, and even my own resistance or curiosity to them interpersonally, was definitely rooted in an idea that we (young girls and women) were not supposed to become like them. But why would that be so bad? Do Black women not experience anger, frustration with the world and with the people in their lives? With each other?

I do believe it's an issue when the *sole* focus of these characters' stories is their role as the sidekick or the sassy friend, or the Black girl with an attitude – but for me, those characters and their stories spoke to a part of my self that I didn't feel like I had permission to express.

It feels easier to categorize characters – and people, really – into heroes that are all good or villains that are all bad, rather than sit with the reality that both exist within each of us simultaneously.

To acknowledge and offer our selves and others grace for the fact that different challenges – pressure, stress, change, discomfort – can bring out more of the latter.

While I guess it often comes down to just being an automatic brain process, I feel like it grossly reduces our own and others' nuance and sense of self in a way that is often self-serving for our internal narratives about our selves and how we extract meaning from our interactions with others.

You can believe that you should be exiled for the fact that there is any bad in you at all, so you lean into the good for belonging and acceptance and praise from others – even your self – and run from the bad so as to not be abandoned by others.

But, unfortunately, you're stuck with your self, and leave your self unable to be at peace and experience that self fully.

* * *

I have always subconsciously rejected the angry Black woman stereotype; I believe my anger renders itself internally more than any type of outward expression of rage.[29]

So I never related to these stereotypes about Black girls having an attitude in a way that was deemed aggressive. Not in that I intentionally tried to separate my self from other Black girls and women because of that (albeit maybe I did subconsciously), I think it's more that – in my attempt to avoid being stereotyped in that way – I cut off a part of my self. I didn't feel entitled to my own anger.

White supremacy, capitalism, and patriarchy all tell us we have to play small, be weak and overly agreeable and compliant in order to have some semblance of safety or progress toward what we think we want in life.

It inherently requires coming out of my self to perform society's ideas of femininity that I – as a Black, dark-skinned, neurodivergent woman – never had access to the possibility of attaining in the first place.

Truthfully, I do oscillate between a desire to indulge in rage and desperation for a safe place to express and process my fear about what that rage – what rejecting patriarchal mandates in both feeling and living – could cost me.

Because a woman without demons is not an angel, she's just not telling the truth. A woman who acknowledges her demons is a crazy, overemotional bitch.

Ambition feels like an endless endeavor to prove to your self and others that the worst parts of you are not all of you. To prove that your worst mistakes just might be outweighed by the height of your potential.

So much of what it means to actually look up to women that are lauded as paragons is to do so without really knowing if how they show up in the world is representative of their truth or if it's a carefully curated shield.

For me, I feel a certain imperative to not allow people to decenter my personhood and humanity from how I show up, the labor that I do or do not do; the ways in which I do, or do not perform my identities for the world.

But what does it actually mean to be a Black woman and assert your self in the world?

Less than childhood trauma, I think that my dilemma in life is that I had a lot of examples of who, and how to be, and it informed a lot of my dreams and set the tone for my imagination.

With that, I think I became hyper-aware of who and what got particular types of attention. It was cheap – and it was disappointing to sometimes see certain women accepting or even vying for it versus fighting for meaningful acknowledgment as human beings.

Notes – undated

Optimal, distinctiveness theory:

- *The balance between distinctiveness and homogeneity*
- *"Brewer asserts that individuals will only define themselves in terms of appropriate social identities that are 'optimally distinctive' and will refuse identities which are either too assimilated or too different."*[30]

"The desire for destruction or revenge." Because you want someone to see you and acknowledge your pain.

Black Women and the superwoman complex:

Notes from The Trap of Thinking You're Special and Entitled to Success[31]*:*

- *Nobody helps the hero because nobody thinks the hero needs help*
- *Not wanting to just be successful, but undeniable*
- *Your POV, value, and how you work with others without degrading or downplaying your self*
- *Uncomfortable to speak like that about my self or my goals, but I also don't want to water down what I believe I'm capable of*
- *It's one thing to say that not everything will work out in your favor, in fact, some things will actually work against you — because that's life. It's another thing to convince your self or others that your perspective, desires, plans, wants, and dreams are too much and that they should be made smaller or*

nonexistent.
- *Endless duck paddling in the water without real movement. Excellence and overworking are not the same thing.*

I have worked hard to excavate my self from underneath all that the world tries to tell me I am and am not. And not (entirely) because Black women are pitted as a societal underdog and because I have something to prove, that's the only model we have for self-preservation (I'd rather use that than 'survival'). I just want to make sure that I am okay and taken care of.

I feel the most misunderstood when people don't take the time to listen to or be curious about my motivations for my decisions and actions, and especially when they villainize me because of what they assume are my motivations.

I think that it has helped...is helping...to evolve toward a mindset of seeing my self as a part of a collective orientation to a common goal through which I can lean on others for support along the way. Rather than overly identifying with my work and my labor, and making everything about my (perceived) performance or how to avoid being a burden to everyone else.

In that, I think it gives me an opportunity to move beyond the egocentrism of being subconsciously driven to prove my self – prove that I am not a bad person who is bad at being a person.

But the caveat with that is: I see now that I'm being invited to let go of being the center of the story – of playing into the narrative that I am this bad person who one day overcomes all of their badness, all of their flaws, and is suddenly and finally recognized as a hero.

With that comes the realization of my shame in the fact that I was never going to live up to that expectation anyway.

I can finally be honest about the fact that, while I know that I'm smart and capable, things have so often felt big and scary and important and more complex than I was built to be able to handle. About how afraid I am of messing everything up.

About how I don't believe I've ever been able to lean on people in my life to help me assuage – or at the very least validate – that fear.

About how, maybe I have prioritized being good and doing a good job, doing good in the world as a way to build equity against my perceived – or maybe my inherent – disposability.

Because at the end of the day – if you're not good for someone's bottom line – even if it's your own – what are you here for?

I often wonder if the women I look(ed) up to ever felt similarly – like they were stuck in a cage in some way, shape, or form – by societal expectations for women around marriage, motherhood, career... existing.

Regardless of where they started out and where they ended

up, the point I believe I took from their stories was not a complete overcorrection in terms of agency, freedom, and independence, but a prioritization to discover my own sense of self. One that I had the space to explore and understand, and having that self be acknowledged and – if not loved and appreciated – respected by others.

It was not being told who I have to be in order to please others – living a life that part of me hates and that feels miserable to be in and live.

It feels like the direction of my life is at the whim of other people's and the world's perspectives of me, and that I don't have the power to inform that so that it is the truth.

We tell our selves and each other to uncritically look at the legacy of "Black Excellence" and "Black Girl Magic" without thinking about the toll it actually takes. Is that who and how they truly wanted to be?

The through line is the even larger social systems that show up in our individual lives. The bigger players that seem to have it in them to constantly play this game day in and day out. When we hold those people in the institutions they represent as our baseline, we fail to consider the reality of who we are and what we're carrying.

Notes on building a life and career as a practice:

- *Moving away from places and things that are devoid of emotion, spirit, and humanity*
- *Fixated on data and numbers – not that it isn't valid, but even when robots take over the world, we will still be spiritual beings having an Earthly human experience*
- *It's all about money, power, and fame. None of it is inherently original – or rather it doesn't inspire you to be original or seek originality. Who and what is supposed to guide you to be rooted and grounded in the truth of who you are – what you know is your work and what is not as you navigate your journey?*
- *For example, it may not actually be about money for money's sake: It may be about needing to prioritize security. and maybe that invites you to see beyond money. maybe that's investing in your relationship to your self your home and your community, your people; and exploring how that can produce stability for you, too.*
- *Maybe it's not about power and fame. Maybe it's about culti-vating a platform that allows you to reach and meaningfully connect with other people.*
- *That feels more intentional and worthwhile than chasing what is cheap and fleeting, often because we aren't connected to something beyond what is immediately in front of us.*

Why does it seem so easy for everyone else to show up and be big? To take up space with clarity and certainty about who you are and why you are here?

Aiming to be enough seems like a bare minimum requirement,

enough by whose standards? It's giving "just enough to get by." It's giving – forcing my self to tolerate my self the way I feel like everyone around me tolerates me, to accept it and view it as a good thing.

I simply did not receive brownie points for simply showing up – which in some ways has served me well, and in others has kept me in a perpetual hamster wheel of perfectionism.

Particularly in moments where the discomfort of things feeling out of my control, in moments where I made mistakes or even caused harm to others (neglected to or unable to hold space or fully see others with kindness, compassion, and in their full humanity and in the nuance of an interaction), or failed and missed a mark.

It feels like the emotional residue that I sit with is about not being seen or acknowledged except for when I made/make a mistake – about how the punishment or retribution for being human always feels a little too harsh.

And it seems as if no matter how you slice it as a Black woman, wherever you aspire to go, you are forced to accept the risk of having to walk that journey alone – unacknowledged and uncared for.

I am working to accept and reconcile my feelings about my own limitations, and my own capacity to hurt and harm other people, as well as my capacity to forgive and heal and move forward without beating my self up about my own judgment.

I have a lot of apprehensions and fear about the person that I might become in a negative way if I don't have control and intervention over my circumstances and reactions to those circumstances. There is fear about accepting and resigning to weakness and inferiority as my truth, while also struggling with my refusal to become a woman that is a caricature and a product of the patriarchal imagination.

I don't want to isolate my self so much but at the same time I don't want to accept weakness and impassivity that can very often be associated with women stereotypically – or align my self with the patriarchal ideals and mandates that say I have to accept this in order to "move forward" and "succeed" in life. I know that is exhausting and I would be miserable; it also keeps me from accessing joy and deep connections.

I would think that not being intentional about the things that you allow to influence and make you without deeper interrogation doesn't seem truly healthy. But all that leaves me is to avoid situations that I think might bring out the worst in me – situations whose outcomes I can't predict all the way through.

As a result, I feel like I'm over-functioning – maybe because of an inability to sit with discomfort and anxiety, and ambiguity about progress in the future. I feel an underlying anxiety and persistent need to overcorrect my self – I never have and likely never will live recklessly to that extent because I always knew I could get hurt or derail my life. I simply retreated and stopped sharing that part of my self – the part with intense wants, needs, desires, and dreams – with others to protect that for my self.

I feel like I'm mentally overcompensating to save everyone and everything from themselves. Or maybe, to save them from having too much of a destructive impact on me.

But I'm done fighting to be seen and heard by people, systems, and institutions that were never interested in seeing and hearing me in the first place.

For self-preservation mainly – but I'm realizing that I don't actually know what it feels like to be seen and heard. Centered. Chosen. Considered. Valued. Invested in.

I don't believe that others have a vested interest in me, my needs, my hopes, and my dreams.

I don't feel connected to true agency and clarity about my own inner voice and individuation. I don't know where others' voices end and mine begins.

I believe that I have a fear of being perceived as a selfish or outright bad person. I think I'm afraid to confront the possibility that my being self-involved, for the sake of self-preservation has negatively impacted other people.

I think I'm afraid that a coping mechanism for the sake of self-preservation has left me even more disconnected from the people around me. That, despite my efforts to continue to show up for my self – even under the guise of showing up for others – has not actually done anything to decrease the mental and emotional chasm that I feel between me and everyone around me.

All that effort, not for nothing, but maybe not for the things I actually needed.

It feels easy to want to double down on the self-victimizing narrative that I must be easy to forget, ignore, not see. And it feels unfair to acknowledge that everyone around me is also dealing with their own stuff and that they just don't have the capacity to hold space for me.

But, either way, fighting in order to be seen and heard is not sustainable for me anymore.

Notes – undated

You can't really blame anyone, person or group of people for your resentment and contempt. Because you internalized all the things that people have said about you and doubled down on that with your own feelings about your self.

Pause and think about the story that you told your self about your own needs, wants, and desires and hold your self responsible and accountable for the fact that it just is and this is where you are. Other people and situations may be a mirror to reflect that back to you, but at the end of the day, you must do your own work.

Desire has always felt a little arrogant to me.

How do you respond when the things that you want, and

desire are made to seem like childish indulgences?

I think a lot about spiritual practices that talk about nothingness – wanting for nothing, and being nothing – as the way to transcend your ego. But I can't help but think that as a Black woman, you are forced into a different kind of nothingness. When that removes your ability to choose to transcend how the world has already defined you.

So it feels weird to try to embody those ideals. Maybe a better first step is to allow my self to first acknowledge and experience the full breadth of my being and wanting instead, pursue nonattachment, and non-judgment to my self in the Universe, regardless of if I receive or become.

I know that I want to receive abundance and to belong without being owned. Maybe the difference lies in your boundaries and your awareness, ensuring you have a full cup to share with others. Knowing that the cup and what you have to share is yours.

Belonging, to me at least, is knowing that I have the space to decide how I want to show up and who I want to be in the role that I have in a certain space and in my life.

* * *

The act of asking for help/seeking support in and of itself is not the issue. A lot of it for me is the *how*.

What specific language do you use to signal to others that you need support emotionally or otherwise without invalidating your self and your experiences, or reinforcing a narrative of helplessness and weakness...laziness and naivety.

I'm very aware that I am a human with limits and that I need support but I'm also protective of my self in that space because people don't take people that hold any of my identities seriously or treat us with softness, care, and dignity.

I'm at a point where being empathetic and considerate towards my own and other humanity and context is not negotiable. I may not need to know everyone's life story – I do think we'd be better for it, but I don't believe that it should be a requirement for basic kindness, care, and respect. that goes for the most personal and intimate of relationships to how that impetus is codified in our social contracts as well as our institutions and policies.

I don't care about performing resilience – because I feel like it reinforces an idea of an inherent deficit, weakness, or incapability. Especially to those who subconsciously or consciously already see me that way and have decided that's all I'm capable of being.

I can also be honest with my self and say that in the moments I did try to express vulnerability – to allow my self to acknowledge and embody that, and to allow others to witness me in that space – I regretted it. Because the emotional residue that I sit with is that they did not respond with kindness and care – whether because of their own capacity or because they did not view me as someone who needed that kindness and care.

And so, for self-preservation, yes it does just feel easier to deal with things by my self. But before you end this essay seeing me for the fearful-avoidant that I am, I also think about and want to bring attention to the inherent assumption that the people right in front of you are or will be the people that show you the most care and compassion.

Staying to my self has also given me the space to center my self and my needs, to self-regulate and re-ground my self. It also gives me the space to see how deeply ingrained that way of being is in so many aspects of society and culture: how we are not afforded the space to truly embody our most authentic thoughts and feelings – for and within our selves, and especially not in our relationships.

It gives me the space to realize I'm not a failure or a bad person – or bad at being a person – because I have found a safer home in my relationship with my self than in my relationships with others.

Most importantly, I've realized that I now have a space to realize that the disconnect lies in trust – or a lack thereof.

I don't think that I trust people to see me and hold me with kindness, care, and respect – particularly in my not knowing. In my internalized and perceived weakness.

I think it's also a deeply rooted scarcity mindset and a fear of losing control – specifically over things that will impact me or represent me (i.e. my work, livelihood, my peace of mind, etc.).

What does it mean to be open to and accept your inherent interconnectedness with others – for better or worse? To accept the inherent truth that you, by design, are a product of the systems and structures that made you. But that you are also a product of your choices?

I don't want to constantly feel like I'm in conflict with other people and the world around me because I feel like I have to or like I should be in agreement or like I am better off minimizing my self to fit and blend better. To not stick out or be viewed as or feel different. To belong.

Instead – I think I want to learn to hold space for tension and contradiction. For my self, and for the people and world around me, and grow to appreciate that tension and contradiction. I want to grow to appreciate who and what taught me and poured into me – because regardless of how I slice it, that did impact who I am and how I move through the world.

It's a balance of honoring your self, not being afraid of friction and conflict that arises from the fact that everyone is different even though we may be similar, and learning to identify and establish boundaries that reflect that.

There's this guise of a rebellion but really it's a flattening and an erasure of my self. An attempt to turn off the parts of me that have some sort of vested interest in that kind of validation.

If I'm honest about the fact that I hate how the world tries to tell you what to think and what to feel, and how to think and feel, and how to speak, and how to move; that will make me less agreeable, less easy, less flat.

It would make me more of a burden. It would cause more friction with the people around me and the spaces I occupy.

If I'm honest about the fact that I find more peace most times when I can be left alone and when I feel like I can take up space in this big world without having to consider other people in ways it feels that they would never consider me, I'm afraid that that makes me selfish.

But if I am not honest – if I continue to not only play this game of playing small, but over-identify with it, and act like I want to play this game of playing small – I reduce who I am and what I want, and I am burdened with offering a version of my self to the world that is not honest.

But it does show me that I am someone that cares more about psychological autonomy – not being contrarian or being different for the sake of it, but priding my self on being clear about what I think, and what I feel so that other people do not rob me of my own process of growth and discovery.

My idea of "don't be a lady be a legend" is more about not being what other people want you to be or what you feel like you have to be but operating and contributing in your own unique way, for your own unique expression of life.

I want to heal, reconcile, and reorient my relationship to and with all the things I am not. I want to be clear about who I am and who I am becoming, and comfortable with all that I am not. Maybe I only want success, because I don't want to be reminded of my past failures – of the fact that maybe I was built to fail. Maybe I only feel driven to put in any kind of work because I don't want to face that if I did nothing else at all, the trajectory of my life would lead to mediocrity and insignificance.

I want to unlearn others' criticism and the world's valuation of what should be standard for women, Black people, neurodivergent people, and young people – all the things that are inherently not me in who I am.

I want to be whole. I want to be all that I am, not all good or all bad, just all of whoever I am in each moment of each day – whether that person got up on the right or wrong side of the bed that day.

You get overwhelmed with the limitlessness of who and how you can be – the good, bad, and indifferent – that you run the risk of getting lost in the noise and missing your inner voice telling you who and how you are.

I know that I don't like being in the spotlight or being seen but there's a part of me that feels like I will miss out on my life and my potential if I don't put my self in positions to be seen. But I don't know that I've prepared my nervous system to understand what that means.

My confidence in my self is something that I've had to work for, cultivate, and earn as I've gotten older.

I want to know what it feels like to take up space within my self – less about commanding an entire room or stadium worth of people, but about being grounded in who I am, where I've been, and where I'm headed. I think sometimes the idea of taking up space seems scary – especially when you've seen so many examples of people "taking up space" when really they are sucking up air.

I don't want to affirm my self for being insecure or having low self-esteem. I want so badly to believe that I am above that or that I can think my way out of feeling those things, not by feeling them or knowledge in them that means I am accepting the least of my self. But it prevents me from being honest and being able to show up honestly.

Accepting failure and weakness – I think people misinterpret where that comes from, not a desire to be that way…to feel and seem tough, but it's just a survival mechanism for self-preservation so the world doesn't take and take and take without supporting, anchoring or fortifying us, or holding safe space for us to let down that guard.

There is so much messaging that you internalize that says who you are is not good enough. not capable enough. That your ideas about who and how to be are fundamentally incorrect.

I desire agency and self-determination over how I invest my time, energy, and essence. Agency in who I am and am becoming.

What does it mean to make sense of my inner power in relation to the world – for that to be self-defined and self-directed? What does it mean to acknowledge that I've been hurt by the world, and by my experiences in it, and to allow my self to just sit in those feelings? And to allow those feelings to be witnessed and acknowledged by others?

Cut You Off (To Grow Closer)

"It struck me that for Black people, the pain of learning that we cannot control our images, how we see our selves (if our vision is not decolonized), or how we are seen is so intense that it rends us. It rips and tears at the seams of our efforts to construct self and identify." – bell hooks, Black Looks (1994)

"I am not my hair
  I am not this skin
  I am not your expectations, no (hey)
  I am not my hair
  I am not this skin
  I am the soul that lives within" – India.Arie, I Am Not My Hair

This is an essay about hair.

It's about how I used to rock rough and stuff with my Afro Puffs.

It's about how, back then, I was free to be a Black girl – I didn't need to have my hair perfectly done all the time or be extra neat. Sometimes I look back at some of my styles and think they were definitely way past well done, but I don't remember feeling too much of the beauty standards a lot of Black girls are subjected to. I remember having fun and doing what I wanted and playing and feeling cute so I didn't really care too much about it.

It's about how I became the little girl with the press and curl.

Grandma took me to get my first perm. It was behind my mama's back, but when I remember how soft and silky my hair felt, I wasn't too mad about that either. I would get my hair done by my Granny's hairdresser during my summers in St. Pete. She was the one who used the shampoo that smelled like Skittles and sold snacks – the one who pressed my hair with the hot combs.

* * *

I think hair for Black children becomes a site of control and lack of autonomy in choosing how to express your self or be given the terrain to try things and embody those phases of interest you may have in childhood, to just be free to be

169

a child as opposed to internalizing the standards that you're being held to when it comes to appearance.

"Just go ahead, let your hair down/You're gonna find your self somewhere, somehow"

I went natural in the fifth grade, I think. I remember doing my hair myself in the mornings – how getting to interact with my own hair and style it how I wanted was my first feeling of true autonomy.

I began to subconsciously (and consciously) reject beauty standards with how I dressed. I was more interested in comfort and doing what I liked and feeling cool or pretty to my own standards.

Sometimes those standards didn't fit other people's standards – specifically of what they thought girls should look like, how girls should dress and wear their hair. I guess that started to get in my head – other people's thoughts and opinions.

"Don't touch my crown"

Even then – I started my locs just so I could leave my head alone and let it be so it could have the space to flourish. That was the first time I gave my self permission to just be – when it came to my hair at least.

I still didn't fit the image of what a girl should be, but I like the freedom of gender expression – although I still identified as a girl, I didn't feel like I was or would ever be entitled to society's idea of femininity externally.

Internally, I was still operating from the expectations that I inferred from what I saw around me. "Why are you this and not that? Why do you look this way? Why are you so difficult to manage sometimes? I'm hard on you because I see who and what you have the potential to be. But you should never sweat, and if you do, I don't want to see you sweat – and you definitely never let them see you sweat."

In the moments when I desired comfort or didn't want to continuously participate in beauty as a project, the world would quickly let me know I didn't fit their image of femininity and young womanhood. And there were moments I was afraid they might actually be right.

Especially now, at this point in my life, it feels like so much of who I've become has been a result of the inadequacy I've felt in my childhood and adolescence, rather than through a lens of opportunity to become someone I'm really proud of and honored to be. How do I work to reframe that lens – to one of abundant opportunity, transformation, and possibility for new beginnings within myself – rather than ceaseless self-correction-and-improvement? Because it has become very tiring, as there will always be another thing.

I've essentially picked up the mantle from all of the people in my life who made me feel I wasn't good enough, and continue to reinforce that story in my own head. Much of that came from the sites of school and work.

I can look back and see the clear breakage between my outer and inner life. What I desperately needed was love, care, ease, and peace, for someone to take the time to truly see and understand me. But that became just another goal to attack rather than one to allow and create space for.

There's a part of me that will always remain true – my essence and spirit – but I don't want to enter the next season of my life still holding on to the mentalities and behaviors that protected my younger self. That said, I still need to take the time to fully address the root issues (my current goal) and create sustainable solutions that account for genuine healing and behavior change, rather than simply demanding that I be better without any substantive support. That is how I reproduce the same voices I'm trying to get away from. That is how we got here.

But this is an essay about hair, remember?

"Let it go/Betcha love can make it better"

This is an essay about how, eventually, I gave up unhealthy striving. Sort of. About how freeing it felt to just up and decide to chop my locs off with a pair of scissors in my dorm room in the Quad and let it all go.

It's about how I finally felt free to start over – this time with the ability to decide how I wanted to show up and who I wanted to be.

Before, beauty came in moments, for special occasions, and for the performance of professionalism. I would usually enjoy the performance in the moment, but having to "perform" all the time is a chore. I hate when beauty and appearance feel like a chore. I hate when it becomes a visible indication of other people or society dictating your expression and how you show up in the world.

If I'm already not who others want me to be – if I've already failed to measure up – what does it mean to fully let everyone down and free my self from that rat race entirely?

Maybe then beauty can become an opportunity to explore and be confident and play, rather than a performance and job and requirement for someone else.

Maybe then I can actually begin to have fun with experimenting with new looks and styles in a way I maybe never allowed my self to before.

I realized I was afraid to try different styles so as to not attract too much attention to myself and not take up too much space. Now beauty is for me to continue experimenting with how I express myself and show up in the world, to continue giving myself permission to let beauty belong to me, for beauty to be rooted in health and wellness, with bursts of expression and experimentation...expansion of the space I take up in the world. It means having fun, enjoying my youth – this body, this being – in the present moment.

173

* * *

There's a lot to be said about how the project of beauty impacts how we perceive our selves and our power, and how others perceive us. Particularly, Black women's power and selfhood seem inextricably tied to our hair. It's the number one predictor of how we might (read: will) be judged by our families, our peers or teachers at school, our employers and coworkers, and our romantic interests. But what do you have to cut off within your self to accomplish that?

Is it patience, kindness, or empathy for your self, and ultimately others? Is it the ability to fully integrate your wounded and authentic selves, and respect and honor your self exactly the way you are in this moment?

Are you trying to aim toward a more idealized version of your self while neglecting the health of your vessel in the present?

Are you waiting for the right place and time to be honest and authentic?

What if you could instead create moments where you can safely be honest with your self about who you are, what you're carrying, and how it impacts how I show up out there?

What if you didn't abandon your self and your body when the reality of being gets uncomfortable?

You don't have to be perfect right now or ever, really. Give your self the room to just be and to grow in your own time.

To be intentional and present with your journey as it unfolds.

Notes – September 13, 2016

Since my freshman year of high school, I've gotten locs, several ear piercings, a tattoo, and then cut all my hair off and expected to feel [more empowered]. But I've willingly and consistently contradicted those acts and given more of my power away by simply refusing to speak. Through other texts we've read, I've realized that by not speaking, not only do I give up my power, I give others the ability to define me for me.

I first read Audre Lorde's "The Transformation of Silence into Language and Action" in a freshman-year English class. That essay was transformational for me for many reasons and as demonstrated here, it showed me how much I pretended that image and my particular attachment to any one hairstyle or color, my piercings, how I dressed, and my one tattoo at the time demonstrated some type of courage or fearlessness in the face of those rigid gender expectations. The whole time, the real journey to understanding true courage, and true personal power, was about finding and using my authentic voice.

So I guess this is actually an essay about how even despite these outward expressions of agency over myself through my relationship with my hair, I was still afraid to show up fully in life.

I absorbed and internalized fear and limiting beliefs about all of the uncertainty, chaos, and pain that is possible in the world. Fear and limiting beliefs about not being able to handle it – being overwhelmed by all of the bad in the world and having that be reflected back to me.

I believe what I care about most in terms of what I want to see when I look at my self is clarity — clarity and confidence in my self-perception. Clarity in my beliefs, thoughts, and emotions. And confidence in knowing what is mine and what is not. Anything else is not my truth and it is not my work.

I feel like I've wrapped a lot of my identity – my sense of who I am and the world around me – in being the kid who always longed. Namely for power, not necessarily over others, but over her self.

I don't want to be that person– it is or is becoming a trope for Black women to be and look successful in winning, but run into the ground and put last in our inner lives and relationships. Who is that for? Who does that serve?

You're afraid of letting people witness you while you're going through a hard time – when you're not perfect. You don't trust people with your vulnerability or your weakness or your imperfection.

I think it goes a lot deeper than simply wanting to experience meaningful connection with other individual human beings. I think that it's about constantly yearning and searching to see your self completely reflected in the world. To not feel alone and like you have to piece together fragments and facets of what you see in the world to make sense of your self and who you're supposed to be.

176

I see how that can feel isolating, until you realize that maybe it is actually your job to dig to your roots to figure out who and what you are, what you need, and how to best foster your growth. And when you find it, maybe it's your job to then express that image in the world – for your self, mainly, and to hopefully offer another fragment for someone to see part of their reflection, too.

And I say a fragment for others, because I don't think that we should be trying to replicate each other's identities and experiences or lives or humanity. It simply just isn't possible. Maybe it's a better use of our time and energy and efforts, to understand our selves for our selves, and to boldly assert that understanding in the world.

Just as I have worked to try and make sense of who I am and who I want to be, with all the pieces of my life that have made up my journey, I think that is a necessary part of the journey for everyone.

Allowing your self to be seen in your vulnerability and weakness allows you to be known, but that reflection back to you makes it real – I think I've been afraid of people reflecting back and kicking up and confirming my own unexamined pain, weakness, failure, and grief.

Grief because I would often feel like it was too late for that version of my self, because I needed that kind of love, care, and tenderness then. Not as much now.

I think I am grieving the versions of myself that were lost

alongside my hope. The parts of me that seem like they hold on to the wrong things for too long may actually be parts of me that are afraid to sit with the discomfort of the reality that I may have to build a new ideal self – a new standard to aim towards – seemingly from scratch.

The part of my self that I've cut off in my own reflection is that I am grieving, and that grief wants to come out and be acknowledged. If I try to tell my self that things aren't as different as they seem just to make myself feel better, I'll enable myself to hold onto old hope. But I feel like I need to grieve and start over with a new kind of hope.

But I see that girl as still a part of me and that I am not over certain experiences. My childhood wounds – and the events that have continued to trigger them – have given me an excuse to continue to intellectualize my pain and disregard my self and my needs in the present moment. Those parts of my self are important and I should still strive to create safe spaces for those parts to be held, healed, and expressed.

I think it's about learning to be deeply, radically vulnerable, and honest. But it's also a practice of sitting beside and not in my feelings (read: being so immersed in my sadness that I make my self and others around me miserable). I have the power to make decisions for my wellness and happiness and peace.

"I'm tryna learn something new/I'm tryna find myself"

This is an apology to my hair...and my self.

I'm sorry I wasn't attuned to what you truly needed. I'm sorry that I didn't speak up when I did become aware of what made me uncomfortable or what I didn't like or when I knew that the way you were being treated – how I was treating you – was wrong.

I've over-internalized and, honestly, overstated, the extent to which your growth was on me. I internalized too much of the pressure and expectation. It didn't allow me to see the opportunity in our interconnection with those around us, and those who came before us.

There are people whose experiences and stories can help you, people who are here and in roles designed to be of support, and people who want to and are open and willing to help. Let them.

I hope you can forgive me for making you feel like you had to be anything other than exactly who you were and are to be cared for and to receive goodness in this life.

I am trying to be more open to the fact that I have more growing to do my self. Now I have the opportunity to rebuild our relationship and grow intentionally with room for learning, mistakes, exploration, and healthy risks. To not feel obligated to engage in surface-level performances of vanity for others.

To, this time, take care of you properly and get out of your way so you can flourish – letting go of all my expectations and assumptions and stories and criticisms – and allow you to just be and see what happens and to try to hope for the best.

III

IDEAL SELF

"If I didn't define myself for myself, I would be crunched into other people's fantasies for me and eaten alive." — Audre Lorde, *Learning from the 60s* (1982)

Because it's better to speak...

"Sadness and grief were acceptable, but there was little space in American society for public expressions of female anger." – Nina Renata Aron, Good Morning, Destroyer of Men's Souls: A Memoir of Women, Addiction, and Love (2020)

"The refusal to feel takes a heavy toll. Not only is there an impoverishment of our emotional and sensory life . . . but this psychic numbing also impedes our capacity to process and respond to information. The energy expended in pushing down despair is diverted from more creative uses, depleting the resilience and imagination needed for fresh visions and strategies." – Joanna Macy, World as Lover, World as Self (1991)

I recently saw this TikTok of a Brené Brown interview, where she talks about identity crisis being more of a slow unraveling than a one-time event or full-on crisis[32]. It made me think of the fact that even though I'd re-enrolled in school, a large part of the puzzle was still missing as it pertained to the question of, "Who am I?" I had done all of this self-exploration and had yet to reconcile with the situation that put me in that position, to begin with. Who's to say I won't end right back up in the same situation? What if I'm unable to return at all? How will I cope with and move forward with that?

The most painful experience one endures on the journey to higher consciousness and enlightenment is reckoning with the ego. At this point in my journey, I've done a lot to heal the deeper insecurities and little "t" traumas, to fully see my self wholly.

When I ended up returning to school in Spring 2020, I was already struggling to regain a sense of inner academic motivation. During my year off, I spent a lot of time recovering from burnout and reflecting on my overall relationship with my academic journey to ensure a smooth transition back to school. My main realization was that I don't believe I've ever found comfort or support in my dynamic with teachers, professors, or advisors. After 12 years of education in public, predominantly white schools, I have yet to master asking for support because I felt like the expectation was to just show up and complete my assignments, to try my best to figure it out and avoid taking resources from another student who may actually need them. I still struggle with not feeling seen or heard, coupled with insecurity in my inability to advocate for my self, even as I approach my last year of undergrad which has only been exacerbated by the COVID-19 pandemic.

Even now that I attend a historically Black university, I still deal with internalized feelings of not knowing how or when to ask for help until things are unavoidably falling apart. Especially in times of crisis like this when everybody is affected to varying degrees, I realized that my current means of navigating my college experience were not sustainable, and certainly not enough to withstand this crisis and the transition to online classes. I didn't feel empowered to communicate to my professors or advisors my lack of confidence in my path to completing my degree a year ago, and I didn't feel empowered to talk to professors about how the pandemic affected me and my ability to complete assignments throughout this semester.

Notes – August 11, 2019

I internalized my educational path as my fault, when in reality I was partly a victim of a higher education system that paints itself as necessary for success in the world without being transparent about its human costs.

I feel like if I no longer had Howard, I would lose everyone's positive perception of me, and everyone would find out that I'm actually not all that special.

The idea of being seen and heard, of knowing that others see your feelings and experiences as valid, seems trivial but is something that directly impacts one's ability to feel empowered and intrinsically believe they are capable of succeeding and coming out on the other side of challenges like our current public health crisis. These are obviously unprecedented times in which many people cannot see what life on the other side looks like, but maintaining rigid expectations and responses at a time that demands innovation, patience, community, and compassion will only ensure the demise of many of the institutions society expects college students to one day inherit and lead. Specifically because of the message they often represent that efficiency comes before humanity.

Only until I learned about the experiences of my peers and the Black journalists and professionals I aspire to be like, did I realize that this problem is symptomatic of larger issues faced by marginalized people in both academia and the workplace. Specifically, I learned that feeling isolated and disempowered (or outright discouraged) to take advantage of the resources purported to exist for our success – assuming you're even aware that such resources exist in the first place – is an experience felt by Black people and people of color everywhere. From educational and career success, social mobility, or even health outcomes for Black COVID-19 patients, this dynamic only guaranteed that more privileged people would thrive while those holding more marginalized identities would just skate by – even and especially to the point of life or death.

What this has shown me (always, but especially in the midst of COVID-19) is that the current educational paradigm is one that rigidly expects students to always push regardless of mental or emotional distress to complete assignments. Academic expectations often don't account for the complex and nuanced human experience of people who are trying their best to succeed within a system that isn't built for all students from all walks of life to actually do so. From parents to teachers alike, the automatic expectation of students to

186

show up, perform, and produce at all times without first holding space to take inventory of our mental, physical, and emotional health, sends the message that our humanity comes secondary to our ability to show up and perform, that our value only lies in what we produce. This is exacerbated by a culture that (I think) also doesn't teach people emotional intelligence and healthy coping skills.

Colleges and universities would be remiss to not consider the fissures long felt by students – only exposed and exacerbated by the COVID-19 pandemic – when developing and executing their plans to reopen. The problem of access in light of increased demand for online engagement, time management in light of more students spending time at home, and academic expectations affirm students' humanity and make them feel seen and their experiences validated.

The Romanticization of Howard University (part two)

I've often thought of Howard existing as two, distinct entities – Howard the business and Howard the community of students and alum. And I'll be honest and say that my relationship with Howard University hasn't always been sweet – my freshman year I literally wrote a blog post titled "The Romanticization of Howard University."[33] I wouldn't refer to it as traumatic, but it did show me a lot about the relationship between an institution and the people within and around it.

"Although his life has been affected by this, it's turning the attention from what the issue, again, is really here: student voices and the fact that students are not happy with the state of the university." – Me, on whole-ass CNN

To this day I don't know how to process the fact that I was a guest on CNN discussing the 2018 Administration Building protest at Howard. I initially went to check out the protest as a possible news story for *The Hilltop*, where I was newly promoted as News Editor. It ended up becoming a five-day occupation – for me, at least. The whole thing went on for about nine days, becoming the longest A-Building occupation in Howard's history [until the Blackburn Takeover in 2021, which lasted around one month].

When I think of what led up to the protest and the events that occurred after, one thing that stands out as a constant is a relationship characterized by the resistance between students and the university. HU Resist, a student-run activist organization committed to organizing for Black liberation on Howard's campus, protested several major Howard events – from James Comey's speech at Convocation, or other direct actions on Howard's campus or in the immediate D.C. community.

I always respected their ability to take up space in a way that directly challenged the unspoken expectation of respectability politics – that deeply informs the University's collective persona, culture, and brand. Most of all, their efforts as an organization seemed to truly be for the benefit of our University and student body – including those who may not have agreed with them (or even those like me who did, but who might've been afraid to put themselves and/or their education on the line) to show it.

It was interesting to later learn about the lineage of student activism at Howard – specifically about the student activists who directly contested Howard's role in the perpetuation of classism and elitism towards its student body and the surrounding Washington, D.C. community.

> "ADRIENNE MANNS-ISRAEL: Well to me Howard was living on, on past reputation, that had really cut off in the 50s they were not addressing current issues, or current problems, it just wasn't there. And in fact the things they had addressed only affected a small minority of Black people, but for concern for the masses, it wasn't there. Concern for...real change wasn't there: that they were concerned with getting something for a few Black people, the talented tenth of DuBois, so they could become rich and wealthy and powerful. But they were not concerned with the rest of us."[34]

Notes – May 13, 2019

Ego death: I want to take care of everyone else because I wasn't given that same treatment. It's a valid response that served me in order to help me "survive," but it has left me, in this moment, overcome with fear at the thought of leaving everything behind in order to become who I know I'm meant to be.

Reflecting on my time working in student government and bringing awareness to issues like sexual violence on Howard's campus, I found to like the educational aspect of advocacy – the part where you can share space, as well as your knowledge and experiences with other human beings, and leave more deeply connected to your community and with an expanded perspective. The part of advocacy and activism that is forward-facing, the part that demands your outside voice and your body on the frontlines...that's the part that scares me.

The first protest I ever attended, during one of my first couple of visits to Howard for freshman orientation, was more of a vigil to honor the life of Philando Castile who was murdered by police during a traffic stop in 2016. Other demonstrations that stick out in my memory include the Women's March (which was kind of a joke, but that's neither here nor there), the March for Our Lives, and the Black Women's March.

What I remember from all of these events was that they were effective ways to take up space and make our voices heard. It was powerful to see all the different people who came out to support the cause of the day, toting their signs illustrated with clever phrases that forced you to reflect on poignant quotes or affirmed solidarity with whatever organization spearheaded the march. The chants and songs we recited made everyone feel a sense of togetherness for a cause much larger than our selves as individuals.

All the things I mentioned before that I loved about marches, were also part of the reason why they're not my ideal strategy for how I believe I can personally be effective. There are people who, unfortunately, attend these events because they're the place to be that day...for clout, to be frank. This is something I continually have to check my self on – to ensure I'm involving my self with the issues and organizations I choose to work with and for because I genuinely believe in them, not just for virtue signaling. The latter distracts from the real work for which some people quite literally sacrifice their blood, sweat, and tears to demonstrate their commitment to building a better world and future for us all.

Nonetheless, I also just didn't necessarily see my self in the imagery of organizers and protesters. I always thought it displays more of an exterior demonstration of strength and power, as opposed to what may lie within someone's interior experience. The inner conviction and strength to manifest that conviction externally.

While I believe I have felt conviction, strength, and power at varying times in my life – that has always just felt different. I always felt different – in that, I always felt that I was not made to be someone who could muster up whatever life force needed to manifest conviction in a way that truly had rippling effects.

I think it's less about image and how I'm perceived, and more about feeling comfortable internally to access a greater sense of confidence and alignment with my vision and purpose, and emotional and motivational resources.

I'm still working to figure out what my role is in all of this, but I believe I have a very naive sense of optimism when it comes to the work I do. There's a part of me that wants to see the good in people, to believe that with work and hope we can change society for the better. But the more I learn and read and listen, it shows how deeply ingrained violence and domination are in our society. These are not things that can or will change with one march, one hashtag, one organization. I believe that opening your eyes to the reality of the world around you and unlearning the narratives that you've been fed in order to maintain that false narrative is a start.

* * *

Mark Bonchek of the Harvard Business Review writes "Unlearning is not about forgetting. It's about the ability to choose an alternative mental model or paradigm. When we learn, we add new skills or knowledge to what we already know. When we unlearn, we step outside the mental model in order to choose a different one."[35]

Although he is referring to marketing and business strategies, Bonchek offers a three-step guide to unlearning that I think can apply here:

1. Recognize that the old mental model is no longer serving you.
2. Find or create a new mental model that can better achieve your goals.
3. Ingrain the new mental habits.

Most of what I had to unlearn revolved around whose responsibility it it to lead change. I would like to think that the social institutions created to make our lives easier would prioritize the wellness and success of the people needed to keep them thriving.

To better understand the purpose and function of a social institution, and because words mean things, let's look at the definition. Here's (a rather lengthy, but effective) one from Jonathan Turner's *The Institutional Order*[36]:

> He defines a social institution as *"a complex of positions, roles, norms and values lodged in particular types of social structures and organizing relatively stable patterns of human activity with respect to fundamental problems in producing life-sustaining resources, in reproducing individuals, and in sustaining viable societal structures within a given environment."*

Now, let's break down each of the many, many parts of this definition with the help of my personal fave, Merriam-Webster and the Open Sociology Dictionary:

"A complex *(noun: a whole of complicated or interrelated parts)* of positions *(also known as social status, our status is society relative to other people. Including race, class, and sex)*, roles *(the behaviors and characteristics associated with a particular status. A person can have one or multiple roles)*, norms *(culturally agreed upon and accepted ways of being, sometimes reflected in moral expectations or laws)* and values[37] *(attributes that render a person or thing as valuable or desirable)* lodged in particular types of social structures and organizing relatively stable patterns of human activity with respect to fundamental problems in producing life-sustaining resources, in reproducing individuals, and in sustaining viable societal structures within a given environment."

Similarly, the purpose or function of education as a social institution, in its purest form, was created to formalize the passing down of knowledge from one generation to the next. Of course, now we know its purpose to mean preparing children and all people for the workforce.

"The educational system helps integrate youth into the economic system, we believe, through a structural correspondence between its social relations and those of production. The structure of social relations in education not only inures the student to the discipline of the workplace, but develops the types of personal demeanor,

modes of self-presentation, self-image, and social-class identification which are the crucial ingredients of job adequacy. Specifically, the social relationships of education – the relationships between administrators and teachers, teachers and students, students and students, and students and their work – replicate the hierarchical division of labor." (Bowles and Gintis 1976:131)[38]

I historically have wanted to be helpful to others, not because I'm a saint, but because I don't know how to tolerate pain and discomfort – my own or other people's. I felt like the weight of my response to pain and discomfort and change was my burden to bear alone.

I always struggled to express my feelings about my experiences because I felt they paled in comparison to those of others. And because school (and now, the workplace) never felt like an appropriate place to take up a lot of emotional real estate. So I eventually learned to internalize and intellectualize and isolate my self to try and be self-sufficient.

As a result of that, I believe a lot of my resentment stemmed from wanting to be seen and heard, held in high regard, and affirmed that I'm not just another face in a sea of other people who are more talented, capable, and visible than I am.

I feel resentment towards those who seem to experience ease and thus success, love, care, and deep and meaningful connections. I resent that I do not feel like I can experience the same without exerting an inordinate amount of energy – not just to achieve or experience but to feel worthy and deserving of achieving and experiencing.

I experience resentment stemming from "they weren't able to help me individually," but when you have the moment of realization that you're not the only one experiencing something challenging or harmful, you realize the source is much broader and has much greater social implications than just your singular experience.

I resent never really feeling seen and accepted and valued in community unless I was showing up as someone who was achieving or good or self-assured.

I resent how very emotionally isolated I felt because I internalized those voices as my own harsh inner critic, and refused to allow my self to be seen in a vulnerable, uncertain space.

I'm afraid to look like I care, to be someone who is not afraid to be clear about what I want out of life, and to act as though that is the case. I don't want people to know that I know they see me as what and who I am – weak and insecure and incapable.

I'm angry and feel powerless to do anything about it – like what happened to me doesn't matter, and that I just have to sit here and deal with it in silence.

Even more so, I felt frustrated with my self that I was not

"strong enough" to deal with certain types of discomfort or pain. That if other people can truly go through the fire and come out stronger, I should be able to get through a little bit of heat and pressure.

Journal – September 19, 2020

I equate my belief in my ability to fundamentally transform, with my belief in the world's ability to fundamentally transform. Which is hard because I don't think I am deeply convinced about my own ability to fundamentally transform – for the better, at least.

And I'm trying to imagine and contribute to building a boundless, new world from the same limited perspective.

I know that I need other people – their talents, intellect, dreams, enthusiasm, etc. – to inspire my own. I need the blueprints disguised as breadcrumbs that our ancestors left for us to build new worlds from.

This journey has shown me that demanding the world change before confronting my own capacity for change is futile. The new world would not be sustainable because there will always be people who remember.

It's not just about political beliefs, labels, public or elected officials, laws, books and news articles. It's about ways of being. We forget we are human beings whose life patterns and needs determine how we organize our selves socially and politically.

With this in mind, it's clear that we live in a society that values prioritizing antiquated norms (because that's the way things have always been) above allowing our selves the space to dream about the possibilities that might lie in what could be.

* * *

"If You Love A Thing, Tell It The Truth"

After my path at Howard, I don't have disdain or resentment for my experience, I love the access, opportunity, relationships, and experiences that Howard offered me. I'm now in a position to see that my life has the potential to be so much bigger than Howard. I have a new North Star.

Since returning, I suppose the duration of my matriculation is to show me that I have much more to learn (inside the classroom, of course, but more so figuratively speaking) and much more to do there.

What I've since learned about advocating for your self and for the world, you can't do the latter without learning how to do the former. In order for your advocacy to be rooted in something, you have to also see your self as worthy of advocating for – even on the smallest of scales – then you recognize the depth of how valuable other human beings are and that they, too, are worth fighting for. It's not just about charity and helping people who you think are less fortunate than you. You recognize that you have to take care of your self so that you're able to make space to help and serve others.

Your life is yours, too.

I think we have to stop associating success with visibility and realize the value in locking in on the work we've been called to do in our respective corners of the world. Of course, a greater level of visibility technically makes it possible to reach more people, but is it really worth it if you overlook the people you cross paths with on the journey there and miss the opportunity to create and experience deep, tangible, and transformative impact? More importantly, is it really worth it if it requires you to overlook your self?

The glitz and glam of visibility are romanticized, but I see the way people in highly visible positions are held under a microscope, their lives heavily dissected by people who have an extremely false sense of entitlement and odd emotional investment in the lives of those they've never met.

That lifestyle seems to be the antithesis of who I currently am – I enjoy helping people, and it gives me a sense of purpose. I don't find it revolutionary or spectacular, by any means, to care about other human beings and to want our world to be better. The premise of my politics and motivations in what I do is to contribute to a world in which everyone knows what grace, kindness, and respect feel like – to the extent that it is codified into our social systems and culture.

I believe so much of our existence involves being insulated in our respective social bubbles, concerned only with "making it" and ignoring any experience or emotion that does not align or otherwise intertwine with it.

My Howard experience, up until this point, has offered me the opportunity to get a taste of what I hope to do for the rest of my life – be a good person and create dope shit. Instead of holding on to my rigid expectations and idealization of what my college years were supposed to look like, I aim to open my mind and spirit to receive whatever it is the Universe wants to teach me through it. I don't think I fully had that realization until right now as I write this but I think I had my mind so set on what Howard was, that I didn't offer it – or my self – any compassion or grace for the possibility that it could evolve.

That's certainly what I've felt about Howard, that it is a bubble that will empower and catalyze you, but if you're not intentional about exploring the world and seeing what else is out there, you begin to believe that the bubble is all there is. Sometimes I believe the appeal of the bubble makes you think you have everything you'll ever need, and that there isn't a reason to depart it, for it offers you plenty already. But in the words of French philosopher Blaise Pascal, "It's better to know something about everything than to know everything about one thing."

Journal – September 20, 2020

Throughout quarantine, I've never been that physically isolated. At the same time, my inner world has transformed infinitely – as I receive new information and examine my own beliefs and assumptions about the world.

The emphasis has always been on going out into the world to change it – but what if we really sat and reflected on what we want our inner worlds to look like?

I'd create a quiet vacuum of an existence where I could read, write, cook, travel, kiki with my girls, spend time with my family, create and just be. Without the demands of school or work killing the vibe because of the underlying fear that if we were to drop our sense of urgency and obligation, to spend more time on the things that truly brought us joy – we'd lose the false sense of stability we had.

In this world, I wouldn't be expected to settle (this part is particularly important to note as a Black woman). Settle in work, in where and how I live, in my relationships. I'd create and live in a world where I'm given the time and space to create the life I want for my self, rather than work against the grain to fight for scraps of that world.

My activism has to look like me going into the world to be and do everything I've been made to feel I couldn't be or have.

Sitting here intellectualizing these issues when they're not in my control is a waste of my time and energy if I'm planning to pursue them alone – where I can start is to be steadfast in my vision for my self and my life and be uncompromising in my pursuit of that vision. It is not something I have to overexplain or justify. I can just be.

Transformation – sustainable, meaningful transformation – isn't proven so when you're screaming and kicking because you eventually grow tired and need to rest. It isn't proven by what's in the news cycle, because they eventually (or rather quickly) move on to the next story. Nor is it proven by what's viral or trending on social media, because that world is a fickle vacuum.

I believe the effect of true change is noted over time, because even when it isn't trending – you're committed to its upward continuity. You're less concerned with pontificating and waxing poetic for other people. Instead, you allow your self the time and space to really sit with the information you receive to self-reflect and understand your role in an interconnected web of other souls who chose to take on this lifetime with you.

What is your responsibility to them (if you believe you have one)? How have you contributed to their marginalization or outright oppression? How will you take responsibility (read: responsibility, not blame) for your ancestors' hand in the shaping of our society? How will you take responsibility for the world we leave to and for those who come after us – those for whom we will be ancestors?

In the midst of the latter questions, one defining difference is that we can receive divine guidance for how we will shape our world from this point forward, and act with faith in this intangible, unforeseen future. However, it is not divine guidance nor hope that will create the world we desperately need to actualize right now. This moment requires commitment and deliberate action.

* * *

I don't understand why or how people can willingly be evil, harmful, or abusive. I think that it's because there's something wrong on a deeper level – which leads me to want to excavate and address any bad thing I think about and perceive within my self.

Because when you know that your truth might have the potential to hurt those around you – seeking the truth then feels optional.

When you have certain goals without interrogation – not as milestones to see how far you can explore your highest potential, but to simply be the person that achieves that thing – you run the risk of abandoning your self and those around you in pursuit of arbitrary things.

In my relationship with my self: part of me feels like I absolutely left my self for dead in pursuit of my own potential. I am now working to address repressed anger that exists because I've abandoned my self in order to meet certain expectations and reach white supremacist, capitalist, and/or patriarchal ideals of success.

I experience anger about wanting to be and do everything – about being humbled by the reality that I have one life and will ultimately have to decide and/or accept who I become. About being almost offended by the possibility of what won't work out. About not knowing if I'll ever be the person that I was working so hard to be, or if I do become that person if it will be worth it when it's all said and done.

This has later led me to try and recall times when I have felt forgotten about, abandoned, or unconsidered, and unvalued. Maybe there is a part of me that has preemptively decided that my duty would be to never abandon anything or anyone ever.

There is a funny-yet-heartbreaking realization I had: I think there's a part of me that is annoyed with/hates/has contempt for my younger self. How hard she was on her self and how she let others' negative perceptions of her (real or imagined) get to her so badly. How she longed for things to be different – maybe not her life or circumstances, but for *her* to be different. how she couldn't allow her self to just be, to hell with what anyone else thought.

I hate the dreams and goals and ambitions she had that I am not burdened with actualizing. because if I don't achieve that, I will have failed her. I hate how much she felt she had to abandon her self to get me here. I hate that I am here – knowing what I know – when she struggled so much with what she did not yet know about her self, life, and the world. I hate that I'm here, but I know I would not be if not for her.

I am afraid of exploiting my own vulnerability because I'm able to hold space for my self and feel my feelings – but only when I'm at my wit's end, when all the factors and conditions are causing me deep discomfort – or when the emotions themselves have come too close to the surface and I can no longer conceal them.

I don't know how to start the process of healing and opening up access to more of my emotions – not exploitation, but dreaming up how to (safely and thoughtfully) be more emotionally expressive for my own healing and to gift my self the opportunity to fully experience my own humanity and open my self up to others to experience the kinds of connections I've always wanted.

I'm able to identify when and how I need support, but it is also often inextricably linked to a compulsive mandate to justify that I am in fact genuinely worthy and in need of said support. because I am a Black neurodivergent woman, which means I must need all the help I can get. But I'm also so capable! I can do it! I've got this! Because Black women are strong and magic!

So in that moment, I am just a human being expressing their human needs – not solely for the ultimate act of transactional support – but rather to be witnessed and a vulnerable moment. Who wants to be fully seen and held with compassion and empathy. Who wants permission to just sit and be present in the feeling and to feel it all the way through.

I'm not able to see how that illustrates the sum total of my relationship with my self. I've internalized the voices of white supremacy, capitalism, misogyny, and patriarchy, and their varying intersections continue to try to convince me that decentering my own humanity was not only expected and assumed, or even in my best interest.

Due to that fact, I don't think I want or need any more dreams, ideas, or ambitions that internally justify my incessant desire for self-abandonment and self-judgment.

And I can no longer avoid my human fallibility – the fact that I do, in fact, have needs, and that there is, in fact, a line in the sand that marks the end of what I am willing and able to accept for my self in my life.

That realization no longer feeds my ego – the part of me that wants to feel and be powerless and helpless to avoid doing the more deep and real work. Because discovering that you actually do have power is not always empowering. When you're aware you have to – or you ought to – stand on that, well that gets into self-respect, which is an entirely different conversation.

Notes – undated

You get exposed to a lot of different people in school, in life – for better, worse, and indifferent. I wish I was taught how to be in spaces with other people and not value the voices of kids who are at the same point in life as I am. How to keep the truth and leave the bullshit. How to realize that a lot of the shit we are on as kids, we regurgitate from what we see at home. Obviously, there's no way for me to have known that as a kid, because I'm still learning to do that now. But all in all, I needed to know more definitively where I ended and the rest of the world began.

As a young Black woman, I know that I don't want to raise or educate my oppressors. It's not just about having access to the same spaces or opportunities as white folks, but sometimes integration and "having a seat at the table" seems like the endgame is to be in shared spaces with people who don't and never will see your humanity.

I don't care and have never cared about the opinions of my higher-ups or authoritative figures – about positioning and lauding them as gatekeepers whom I have to shuck and jive for to gain any kind of access, happiness, fulfillment.

I believe the better path is to honor and respect those who came before you and paved the way for you, learning and studying from them. There is a difference. I am somewhat more available to care about what my peers think of me because we're all coming up in these spaces together. But I am learning to divest from acknowledging the white gaze and focusing on investing in how I learn from, serve, and be in community better with Black folks.

I always waited for the moment someone would look at me and say that you and what you're going through are normal and okay. I wanted someone to look me in the face and tell me that I – my qualities and experiences and thoughts and feelings – matter just as much as everyone else's.

To let me know that it's understandable that because of the way my life has played out this far – I, by default, do not always feel safe betting on or waiting for life (and subsequently, other people, spaces, and institutions) to see and hold space for me.

To understand why I'd struggle with identifying whether or how much of my motivation comes from needing to prove something to those people, spaces, and institutions; or from experiencing sincere security with my own distinct path.

Constantly forcing my self to push past my comfort zone in a way that wasn't gentle with my nervous system couldn't have ever been sustainable. Why be vulnerable and feel uncomfortable emotions when you could just identify the problem and fix it?

Because I felt like I would be accepting weakness and inferiority if I acknowledged that some of my experiences – namely resulting from my social identities – were getting to me. So became the person who didn't need support, or needed way less support than everyone else.

That has led me here – trying to grapple with my own complicity, its impacts on all aspects of my life in very real and palpable ways. With very tangible remnants of all that racial capitalism takes from us – in my nervous system, my body, my relationships. It has led me to have to go back and begin that work of internal repair and reconciliation.

As long as this future version of my self exists in my mind – free of the consequences and limits of her own identities and shortcomings – the present version of my self – the only one who is real – will never know true freedom. But I find solace in knowing my disappointment and grief about that fact points me to what I value, what my priorities are.

Then I think, "Who would I be to call my self an advocate for any form of Black Liberation when I have allowed my self to become my own oppressor?"

Believing that having wants and needs creates a burden for others (including for your self) can make it easier to ignore, avoid, or undermine your humanity. Rather than standing in the truth of your desires – only to face the reality that you might not ever realize it, but to still believe that you're worthy enough of the pursuit anyways.

It makes it easy to get overwhelmed by your own needs, as

well as that of others: When you get a moment, not to find refuge above water, but to briefly get a look at another above sea level you realize that they, too, are drowning – both of you struggling to latch on to something bigger and more stable than both of you. You recognize the impact of the world and its systems on other people in the institutions we have to navigate.

How do I continue to manage my self while I continue to do the work and make progress toward those personal and collective dreams? I'm beginning to see that it's about emotional regulation and grounding to at least keep your self level-headed along your path.

If I believe other people are deserving of those things – why don't I feel fully embodied in the fact that, by virtue of my also being human, I am also deserving of my humanity being recognized? What does that feel like in my body to have my humanity fully honored by my self and others?

We can instead imagine working towards the future where we try our hardest to keep our heads afloat while helping those around us do the same. And we can use those collective networks and communities we built to turn our energy and attention toward the larger systems and work to change them together.

The freedom, ease, peace, and liberation you hope for others to have and experience – can also apply to you, too. And when there is nothing left to learn, no more benchmarks to hit, no more goals to accomplish, all there is left to do is to feel. Feel our way into a different reality while waiting for an ever-elusive external transformation in our lives and world.

Notes – Love as the Practice of Freedom

"In World as Lover; World as Self, *Joanna Macy emphasizes in her chapter on 'Despair Work' that 'the refusal to feel takes a heavy toll. Not only is there an impoverishment of our emotional and sensory life . . . but this psychic numbing also impedes our capacity to process and respond to information. The energy expended in pushing down despair is diverted from more creative uses, depleting the resilience and imagination needed for fresh visions and strategies.'*

If Black folks are to move forward in our struggle for liberation, we must confront the legacy of this unreconciled grief, for it has been the breeding ground for profound nihilistic despair." – Love as the Practice of Freedom *by bell hooks* [39]

Break up letter to my Protector

Maybe it's scary because you can't imagine an existence made up of anything other than this.

210

I really try to make it work so I don't think it's about my capability or lack thereof to go to life. I just don't think it's meant to be here. I thought that would feel exciting and hopeful, but I instead feel really guilty and maybe even disappointed that I couldn't be happy with what I have already.

You feel guilty for having wants and dreams and desires. For seeing something beyond was immediately in front of you because parts of that just are in other parts of it or what someone else had to offer you. So you feel guilty for saying that that isn't enough.

I don't think that I am someone who wants a lot for the sake of having a lot, nor am I someone who wants a little because I'm okay with accepting the least from this life. I recognize my habit of being okay with less because it makes it easier for those around me. And I also would like to know that more is accessible, regardless of who or what facilitates that for me.

What I'm no longer accepting is people trying to tell me what it is that I want or what it is that I should be okay with because of what is in their capacity. Or trying to encroach on my process of holding space for and listening to myself to get clarity on what it is that I want and don't want.

Because I have taken the time to get to know myself, and because I am the only one in my life who has a central vantage point on myself in my life, I am the only one who can provide the information about what I have the capacity for, period, the capacity I have to be stretched and challenged, or if I'm in a season of just wanting to rest and have my cup filled – rather than one of doing and pursuing and filling others cups.

I believe self-betrayal comes when I ignore that inner knowing and prioritize what I assume others might expect from me.

Maybe right now I do not represent stable ground for others because I'm in a space of constantly attempting to reconcile what is what I actually want to do and what I feel like I have to do – trying to reconcile desire and obligation.

It may be that obligation is subconsciously assumed to keep everyone around you from ever feeling bad if you can help it. But what has come at the expense of that obligation is your own ability to speak your truth about how other people or circumstances or experiences have negatively impacted you. Or your ability to express your interest in and desire for more for your self and your life.

I don't know if my "people-pleasing" tendencies have come from a sincere desire to please other people. I think that I have internalized the pressure to be this altruistic, successful, and loved woman. But I don't know if I have been honest with myself about the reality of what that really requires.

What is the reward that you're looking for at the end of all of this?

Maybe it's that at the end of it, all you feel is the subconsciously-assumed obligation to prevent your self from feeling bad. A sincere belief that being the altruistic, successful, and loved woman will protect you from the worst the world has to offer – and maybe what you perceive as the worst is just the grand yet purposeless uncertainty that is inherent to living.

And maybe, in terms of how you relate to others in the world around you, you subconsciously assume the obligation to protect others, from the truth of how you feel. That you should shoulder the weight and impact of your emotions alone.

I don't think that desiring to be altruistic, successful, and loved is inherently a bad thing. But what happens if you don't achieve that?

And when you've already started to build a foundation off of that pursuit, what happens when you want to start again?

It almost feels like it would be dishonest to abandon all of the work I've done up until this point and disrespectful to all the previous versions of myself that worked to get me here.

But it would also be dishonest if I continue to carry on the burden of that work, knowing that I changed my mind. To continue to bear the weight of a shell that was long-hardened but never full. A shell whose true contents have finally surrendered to just being enough, rather than allowing itself to remain stuck in a fruitless pursuit to fill itself up.

What if it's actually not anyone else's fault or responsibility? What if you're meant to simply start with the truth of how you feel? Where might you be able to go from there?

* * *

Audre Lorde's *A Litany for Survival*[40] continues to be that anchor for me, and I've been exploring her works – again including the essay "The Transformation of Silence into Language and Action"[41] – outside of a sociopolitical context. Namely, to think about what it means to speak up for my self with regard to my emotions and human needs.

On making my voice heard is an act of self-love:

- I built a cage for my self and called that success – and now I have resentment towards my past self for not acknowledging and expressing my needs and my limits earlier.
- I don't want to just be coddled and told that life will work out (just to avoid the reality of hard or uncomfortable things) even if I believe and trust and have faith that they will. I want to feel competent and trust my self to know that I can face and hold space for my self to deal with the inevitable discomfort and disappointment inherent to life.
- I am learning to accept that I have needs – that I am and will always have needs; but that I have the power to start where I am to begin to meet those needs and care for my self.

I'm very quick to abandon of the good things I want – with no fight or effort – if I realize it may not really be for me, or if it seems like it *might* be difficult. But what *is* for me? What can I look forward to?

I know this is more of a question for God than anyone or anything else. But I know that I've been blessed in this life. I'll be okay if I don't experience another good thing, and I will

214

continue to be and do good to the best of my ability.

I struggle with the idea of people-pleasing, and "being a good person" to demonstrate what I want to experience, to achieve safety, belonging, etc. I know that regardless, I shouldn't live that way, and so there's something that becomes resistant to that when thinking about my own wants and needs for my self in this life. But I also feel like I'm meant to offer more than solely living for my self.

Much of my learning and understanding about power dynamics and self-advocacy has led me to feel like it is me against the world in my journey to reconcile a lot of the powerlessness I felt as a young girl. I recognize that to heal that relationship with my inner self I have to be the advocate for my self that I wish I had for my younger self.

That involves holding space to really understand what is really going on and giving my self the space to just be in my feelings. That doesn't mean automatically jumping into the solution, that's spiritual bypassing and toxic positivity. And it doesn't mean nonattachment because that turns to avoidance.

But it also doesn't mean that I instead have to sit so heavily in my emotions and stay there in the name of giving those emotions the space they didn't receive in the past. I have enough self-awareness to know how to describe my emotions and where they come from. I also have enough self-awareness to know that staying buried in my feelings doesn't serve my higher self and where she's trying to go.

So part of my self-advocacy also involves holding that space for me to fully name and sit with and process my emotions and experiences and thoughts. I believe the next step of growth is to learn how to let it go.

The work I need to do is less about continuing to acquire more knowledge and information, but to do the internal work needed to shift my perception of my self and my capacity to lead transformation in my life and in my corner of the world.

How the people and environments I've been in have contributed to my not feeling confident in my self as a leader. A lot has undermined my ability to truly see my self as someone who is capable of being and becoming my best self – criticizing things that are inherent to who I am that I can't change. Things that – if they were to change – I'd feel like I'd lose in favor of something that doesn't deeply align with my true values and purpose.

*　*　*

Break up with the version of your self that is and was afraid to speak up. She helped you survive up until this point, even though she also put ego over true vulnerability and connection. She kept you dreaming and connected to the bigger picture. She wanted nothing but the best for you.

Instead of minimizing her response to negative or hurtful things she experienced, and creating an internal narrative of self-victimization, learn how you can become your own savior. Not in that you're self-sufficient to the point of not eating anyone at all, but so that you can have space to show up for others and serve others while having done the work to know and understand your own needs and how you desire others to show up for you.

It's easy to get lost in broader social issues and experiences – as we aren't taught, given the time and space, or otherwise incentivized culturally to sit squarely and deeply with our selves and our own lives.

People just become aware of their emotions, they don't do the subsequent – some might say maybe even more important – work to actually process and feel their emotions (and the emotional residue of their past) with the goal of alchemizing and transmuting them into a greater vision for how they experience themselves and how that impacts their experiences with the world around them and others in it.

I'll do my part but these social systems, institutions, jobs/companies/organizations, people – even my own limiting beliefs, ego, dreams – do not own me.

I believe that there are larger systems and structures that need to be enforced and reinforced, systems of care and providing resources to meet peoples' needs in order for them to show up. I believe that there needs to be alignment on shared values, visions, and goals. When those things are missing, I believe it creates power dynamics where those with more power and privilege get to decide what the goals and outcomes are, and where people with less power and privilege have to bend to those whims in order to feel like they're making progress or to succeed. These dynamics often are not driven by our own sense of internal knowledge and collaborative ways of approaching life, relationships, work, etc.

Rarely do we create time and space where we ask our selves and each other what we truly want and need and desire before immediately feeling compelled towards uninformed action. These dynamics – capitalism all the way down to our interpersonal relationships – sometimes rely on us not knowing who we are and what we want. Because for them, manipulation and control are easier than taking the true time and space needed to discover and honor each of our respective humanities.

I believe that we are all experts in our own lives. With that, I've tried to unlearn my understanding of empathy as trying to put my self in your shoes as if I could ever know what your experience is like. I'm learning that empathy is really about holding space for someone to share their experience with you – to first prioritize the work of being a safe and worthy space for that sharing and then to actually give a fuck about what they have to say if and when they share with you.

The former centers your self and arrogantly assumes that you have an all-illuminating awareness about things you literally might not have gone through. Allow people to just tell you about their journeys themselves. And actively listen to what they have to say.

To Howard, My Unrequited Love

"When you invest in a seed, watching it grow without you, that is a bitter pill to swallow. Sometimes you need to feel the pain and sting of defeat to activate the real passion and purpose that God predestined inside of you."
– Chadwick Boseman (2018)

"The Institution cannot love you." – Tressie McMillan Cottom

To Howard, my unrequited love:

You were my dream, my North Star, for so long. You were my license to aspire and demand more of and for my self. I immersed my self in you and the experience you've gifted so many, for so long. After leaving, I got to a point where I felt I'd gotten everything you were meant to give me, and that if I had to leave without closure, our experience had served its purpose.

What are you supposed to do when you put all of your hopes

and dreams into a thing – entrusting it to hold them carefully and see them through to fruition, only for it to release its grip on them when its interests, hopes, and ambitions come back into its front of mind.

Are you forced to accept that maybe it only held onto you and your hopes because it had a little bit of time and space to spare? Do you embrace the shame that comes from realizing that you needed it more than it needed you? That it was – for a moment – one of the few places you could see a sliver of hope for your self and your life path to possibly be and become something much better, much bigger than who and what you were before you crossed its path.

I keep thinking. About whether I'll ever see you again or whether, at the bare minimum, I'll ever get proper closure. And I guess the situation wasn't deep enough to warrant any of this. Or, well, that's the story I tell my self to minimize my feelings, and somehow excuse the basic common decency that I feel like I deserved. Part of me just does not fuck with you in the slightest, but the other part of me, the majority part, just wants to know why.

I guess it was cute at first, but 3 years later I feel like I've kept my self stuck. I feel like I've wasted away my time hopefully waiting on something that was never going to happen. I got caught up in the promise of love and the hope that I thought you would bring it to me.

I guess I have to accept the fact that my heart and my hope were shattered a long time ago, and that a part of me still felt the need to hold out for that promise.

* * *

I went back after a year and during that year I did the work –
worked on my self, found hobbies, and reconnected with my
self. When I went back, we weren't the same the second time
around.

I'd hoped for a more ceremonious reconnection and acknowledgment of where I'd been and how I'd changed. But it was
just back to business as usual.

Why don't you see me? Do you see me? Have you ever? I
don't want to assume. I know life is overwhelming for all of
us, but I believe I deserve to be seen by someone. Or at the
very least feel seen. If only by my self.

To do that, though, I'd have to acknowledge the fact that
there's a part of me who feels like her life is without meaning
– filled with these sparse magical moments but nonetheless
boring and normal in the in-between moments. I'm having
to unlearn that life is, in fact, not a romantic drama – but that
doesn't negate my desire for a magical, but more importantly
meaningful, life. I want it to mean and have meant something.

I think the issue is that I get stuck in this space of longing,
as there's no concrete information that would definitively
lead me to believe that there's no chance of anything magical
happening...or any chance of that magic staying. There's no
way for me to definitively say that.

I think this is also in part to the need to find proper closure – which is a functioning brain process, not something that I can control as the brain feels more comfortable after finding a proper "end" to a story or narrative. When that doesn't happen and there is seemingly a gap left in the situation, the brain doesn't process everything clearly and still longs for whatever is missing or just generally longs for a more conclusive ending to the "story."

Continuing to operate from this place of longing and constant anxiety that derives from it comes from the fact that reality and my perception of it are not matching up. Especially when you sit in this place of longing without understanding what you'd be getting into if your idealized outcome came to fruition.

The point is not the outcome, but rather the process – the fact that I am not going to be unapologetic about what I want and that I am 100% willing to try to see if it's a possibility (and act on it if it is), knowing that I could very well fail. I think shying away from the situation or trying to act like I don't really care, will only leave me feeling regret and anxiety from sitting squarely (and cowardly) in this place of believing, but not acting. And I think where I get stuck is in the place of knowing all of this and being ready and willing to try, but not actively seeking (or taking advantage of) an opportunity to act or make a decision. I think not forcing it but being very clear and distinct about taking heed of opportunities will get me where I want to go (in addition to actually setting my self up to be successful instead of doing the opposite as a manifestation of expecting to fail, and allowing the inevitable failure to confirm that expectation).

Again, in general, but with this situation specifically, it's not about you or about arriving at an ideal outcome. I think it's about me prioritizing the work of maintaining ownership and responsibility over my feelings about my experiences.

It's not about me employing the "by any means necessary" mentality – specifically by participating in obsessive, faulty, or otherwise inauthentic practices or ideals – just to arrive at my idealized outcome. It's not about forcing the situation in either direction (i.e. self-sabotaging or rushing through the stages needed to build a sustainable foundation). It's not about allowing external perceptions of my situation, or my thoughts and emotions to dictate how I should feel or what I should think. While other people can provide additional information or objective opinions of my situation, I should only allow that to inform or support my final decision – not dictate it altogether.

Notes – undated

Love should be the one pure and innocent thing.

But what happens when you put the promise of love as salvation above your peace of mind in the present?

If and when I do arrive at that promise, I will resent my self, my life and everyone around me.

I want to believe in love so badly

But not at the expense of my self in the present

I want to simply be allowed to love a thing

Until it feels foolish

I guess that I never thought of love as the receiving, just as the opportunity to love and feel and give into that feeling fully

The desire for redemption and salvation disguised as the promise to love

What do you do when the things you choose don't choose you back?

You broke my heart, you know. From putting all my hopes and dreams into the idea of you and the promise that idea offered to me and everyone who crossed your path. From feeling safe enough to take that idea, that promise, and envision a version of my self that was made fully better by it.

The version of my self that arrived here was not afraid to dream and imagine and embody the worlds of possibilities around her. The version that left? The version that left? She experienced her world of safety and comfort collapse and desperately tried to put the pieces back together to give her self some safety in an illusion that nothing had ever happened, that she hadn't missed a beat.

She thought she was someone who knew, someone who had to see for her self to be able to decide whether it was or was not for her. Who felt like she had the power to choose her destiny because you gave her permission and a safe space to believe that.

Maybe we are who and where we are because life was just meant to be that way.

It feels like, with you went my ability to put my hope in something, even though deep down a part of me knows you may have never been equipped to hold that hope and make something useful of it.

I pedestalized you, I see that now. And I don't know for sure if there's a part of me that is still waiting for the day you reciprocate that.

I guess I could continue to wait and hope and depend on the circumstances changing or for the timing to be better. But even if it did, what do I expect to happen then?

It makes you almost wish the good moments didn't happen at all, just because it gave you a glimmer of hope that better... more...was actually possible.

A part of me knows that I am or will be okay without you. I think the friction comes with acknowledging that maybe I never really had you at all. And that the potential I felt to create or discover a new self-definition was never because of you to begin with.

Note to self: Don't build and invest in worlds around hope.

Hope was never meant to be the foundation, but rather a guiding light.

When hopes and dreams do more harm than good, you can't be present and meet your self where you are because your hope has turned longing and dreams into escapism.

* * *

While love has been the container for many of my hopes and dreams, more often than not it has also been the primary catalyst for my disappointment and heartbreak and grief. I'm ready to acknowledge that now.

Maybe I broke my own heart by expecting so much from life. Even if it started in good faith, my hopes turned into uncompromising expectations upon which my happiness and fulfillment were contingent.

I needed you to protect me from the discomfort brought by my fear that reality will not follow a perfect, pre-rehearsed script. I needed you to be the 'villain' in my story. I needed it to be that easy.

You never stood a chance against my mountain-high expectations. Having to leave shattered my naïve expectations open about the world in a way that I wouldn't have had the courage to do my self.

This realization seems shitty, but it does help me better situate my self with how I relate to the world around me more authentically. Here, I can be honest about where I feel vulnerable and less than. Here, I have something to work with. Here, we can get into alchemy – rather than avoidance or wishful thinking or hopeless pessimism.

What happens if I never get those things? Who am I then? Who am I without the potential versions of you subsidizing your worth in the present moment?

What if I just sat in this really gross feeling of not being good enough? Of not having hope or surrendering to the fact that I will never get my happy ending. What happens then?

Maybe what I'm feeling is grief for the thing I hoped and longed and dreamt for, and for the part of me that was capable and eager to hope and long and dream.

But I don't know if that gives me the power to overcome the grief of what I've wrapped my hopes and aspirations around.

I'm grieving the fact that the former version of my self – and who I imagined I'd become – will never be fully realized.

I'm grieving the idea of love and life as I previously understood it to be. The version of my self who was longing for a concept of love and life that I have outgrown.

I'm grieving the possibility of experiencing the fulfillment of something long hoped for, rather than facing the reality of what is in my power to intentionally and carefully build and cultivate.

I'm grieving all the possibilities of what I could have been. All the versions of my self that entertained the possibility that you were my one.

I'm sitting with an accumulation of all this grief – which I feel much more deeply than possibility and potential. I guess to do well in life you have to get good at grief, too.

* * *

Who and what do we idealize as the only possible containers for our potential?

I'm learning how to find love from an abundance of places so that I don't waste my numbered days waiting on you.

It's about holding space to repair my relationship with my self, with time, my intuition, and my trust in my ability to safely hope and dream.

Fulfillment, meaningful progress and evolution, and connection have always been my North Star. Not surface-level and transactional relationships, or vanity metrics of success.

In who and what do you put your faith? Do I have faith in my self?

In that space – the pause before the answer – there is freedom. Freedom to be, to allow my self to imagine beyond the confines of what I think I should want to do or be.

228

There I find space to simply exist – to look at your self and the world and your little existence in it. And just be. But in that space of simply existing, are you happy with who you are? Do you accept where you're at in your life at this very moment?

Coming to that realization as well as the realization that I was forcing and rushing everything because I don't know that I trust life and the Universe to make space for me and my needs and wants and hopes and dreams.

I was used to not being that girl – not about minor rejections – but about major existential ones. Ones that tell you *"Not only is it not going to be me it's not going to be ever."*

I placed more emphasis on and attached more to the idea of who I could become as a result of being connected to you, rather than a grounding in the reality of what it means to be connected to you. I believe now that it's meant to be a mutual exchange of energy influenced by our current time and space.

I can step back and say that the hope that I see in and through you is a result of the potential that exists within me. I am learning what it means to know and feel comfortable in what I have to offer in a way that doesn't engulf me with you, but that allows me to maintain my agency while leaving room for influence and co-creation.

I'm still afraid that the "what if" will haunt me forever, the years lost, and the fear of being haunted by the ghost of something you couldn't see all the way through.

229

I only found bits and pieces of what I thought I wanted and needed here, and that's okay. I'll hold on to what I did receive, and go on with my life. One way or another.

Maybe I'm putting those pieces together to build my ideal self and life. Maybe it's about uncovering what isn't me to uncover my personal truth.

Because what if you are never chosen? What kind of person will you be and become as a result of that? Of the challenges and uncertainty you face in your life journey?

What does one inspire in you at this period in your life? How do they point a light towards what you need and most deeply desire – rather than transactionally seeking out the answer to "What are they doing for me and what can I get from them?"

I think that we can be aware of the relationship we have with others and even our selves. We capture a still image of them in our minds – a singular image colored over time by patterned experiences – and then hold them to that image as a standard in our subsequent interactions. When they make small, fleeting attempts to change or evolve naturally as all beings do, we discredit them, reserve our praise – or conversely, we drown them in it.

The difference is that you might be able to look at who they are outside of you and appreciate them whether you benefit from them or not.

You can either continue to contort your self to seem more

choosable, or you can choose your self.

I start to try and find my own path outside of you – even being inspired by you – as I'm putting my self and my purpose first.

It feels forced and cliche – like I'm just following the self-help checklist to make my self feel better.

Then, I realize that I *am* growing and learning and moving on. I can't hold on to the idea of us while time continues to pass and I remain stagnant while you go on and continue along your journey.

At some point, you decide it's not worth it to wait passively for someone to save you from the proverbial tower. You don't know if or when you will make your escape and step into your newfound freedom, but you are also definitely clear that you are not bidding on someone to save you *for* you. You decide and you make a plan to move forward with your life regardless of the outcome.

And maybe even worse – what if you're meant to release your persistent hopes that there is something still to be done to change or somehow reverse what has already occurred? I don't need or want to be saved.

I really want it – but not at the expense of choosing the outright wrong thing, or trying to contort my self to fit things that don't fit anymore.

Maybe I'm afraid and overly open because of what I don't

know: *"If not that then what is actually for me?"*

One scenario is that nothing is. Another scenario is that everything is, that you actually have endless options – which is overwhelming.

Maybe there is an unknown, third scenario where I am well on the way towards what is meant for me – but perhaps not in the timing or package I envisioned.

While there is a part of me who of course is hoping for some version of that fairytale ending, there's another part of me who subconsciously feels like I need to know what it feels like to not have something work out in my favor to not get what I dream of.

Maybe this is further intellectualizing to avoid sitting in the discomfort of uncertainty.

And instead of running from that, maybe the best alternative is to simply stand in the truth of how I feel, without over-identifying with it either way and being overly attached to the outcome.

* * *

To Howard, my unrequited love.

I feel like I will always have a soft spot for you because of the potential of how things could have been. Maybe because, after all of this time, I still believe that we might be able to come back around.

But what I can do, in this moment, is instead decide to let go of old feelings and dreams to make room for new ones. To let the idea of love go, and see who or what I might be able to find in the empty space.

Axis Mundi

"When we live outside our selves, and by that I mean on external directives only rather than from our internal knowledge and needs, when we live away from those erotic guides from within our selves, then our lives are limited by external and alien forms, and we conform to the needs of a structure that is not based on human need, let alone the individual's. But when we begin to live from within outward, and allowing that power to inform and illuminate our actions upon the world around us, then we begin to recognize our deepest feelings." – Audre Lorde, Uses of the Erotic: The Erotic as Power (1978)

"I am not the center of the Universe, but I am the center of mine." – Unknown

I've actually been pretty content with my life so far – I think that the constant possibility of "well, what if there's more?" is what bothers me. I'm afraid that – without realizing it – I'm actually on a path to just being the person whose life is just a series of checked boxes.

However, I didn't always feel confident about or secure with the life I was given, and I constantly longed for another place, thing, or person to be worthy of claiming and feeling good about claiming. Things I could feel good about being connected to.

For example, The idea of "home" has always been a tricky thing for me. My hometown of Acworth, Georgia – the City of Lakes and Trains…Trains by the Lake? Anywho – I know we are known for lakes and we are also known for trains.

It's a medium-sized city (not a small town like I previously thought) and for the most part, always felt like a safe place to live, but that was about it. It's a place that reminds you that while there will always be deaths and births, taxes and wars – the most constant thing about this world is the monotony of suburban life.

With my family not being from here, I can't say that I ever felt meaningfully connected to the surrounding community. Not in a way that made me feel similar to other people in the experience of being able to proudly rep your hometown.

What I will say, though, is that I didn't feel connected to a broader collective identity in my hometown, namely its Black history and culture. I always felt more connected to where my parents grew up, because of the perception of that shared history.

For many Black Americans – church is a home, an anchor: I didn't really have a church in my hometown. Most of my church experiences growing up were with my grandparents at the churches they attended in Atlanta, at the Florida church my Granny still attends and leads in (also where my parents met, and where I was Christened), or at the church our family leads in and still attends in Nebraska.

Maybe this is dramatic, but it seems to have reinforced an identity of smallness, non-specialness, and mundaneness. An idea that the places where I was and could be meaningfully connected were always somewhere else, somewhere far.

However, I don't look at my experience in my hometown compared to others and feel like I missed out on anything. I guess it just offered another way to possibly live and be. I know now that I deeply enjoy and need peace and quiet, meaningful connections with others, a deep relationship to and with my self – to remain intuitively aware of what I need and when, when to go out and be and when to stay in and be. I guess small towns make that easy.

I will always need those quiet and still places to retreat to. How can I find balance with that? In the grounding, exploring, and connecting?

Notes – undated

What does it mean to not just physically go back to where you came from, but to recall and reclaim who you have always been and where you have always come from? To remedy being lost in the noise of possibility by refocusing and recentering?

What does it mean to get quiet and reorient your self – forgoing the searching and yearning and dreaming for a moment, so that you can have peace?

When you put so much pressure on moments when things feel too small and still and quiet – how are you expecting to feel? What are you expecting to happen?

I almost feel like I had to carve out such a small space to develop my self-confidence by my own standards – in my room, in the car, in the shower, or in my writing. When my space became more and more internally clear and expansive, I felt friction with others and amplified it fighting to be seen and heard by my own standards.

It seems as if there are so many people and institutions who feel unjustifiably empowered to define you – your character, your motivations – especially with little to no context about who you are and where you came from. About what it took for you to be here.

And maybe it's negative confirmation bias – further reinforcing my fears that making mistakes and not knowing makes me a bad person. I also am left feeling like I'm not given a chance to prove or explain my self. And maybe that is the genesis of the mentality that is holding me back now.

There's an assumption that whatever someone else does to us is a reflection that they don't care or are a bad person altogether. That the only active intentions are bad ones.

We are usually able to look inward and understand our own

context because of our vantage point in our own lives. Maybe since we don't always have that kind of proximity and access to others we subconsciously fill in the gaps.

I've struggled with feeling like I have to care and be deeply emotionally involved with everything. I care about being a good person – rather a person with a solid moral compass that puts humanity above extraction and domination.

I think that I've struggled with subconsciously believing that aim – of being so deeply concerned and emotionally invested – only applied to others and had to come at my expense.

Or maybe that was simply the result of not knowing what it meant and felt like to center my needs, wants, and desires.

Or maybe I noticed and internalized how I thought people felt about me when I seemed unsure, and even when I seemed too sure.

I don't think it's the absolute of either total knowing or total not knowing, but the lack of regard for the in-between. When you're inching towards knowing a little bit more. Circling through certainty and precariousness.

Maybe there are people who truly do come into the world and into themselves with a confident and secure orientation towards their own disposition on that spectrum. Those who are able to build their lives, relationships, and careers from that confident and secure place.

What I do know is that there are others (or maybe I really am alone in this experience) who have been left feeling deeply insecure and vulnerable in that space of not knowing enough.

There are some people who come from that place of perceived not knowing, putting an inordinate amount of time and energy into the pursuit of more knowledge and experience and awareness. To get closer to being someone who knows.

And when this way of being bleeds you mentally and keeps you from being meaningfully connected to others – you realize that journey would be and is endless and futile. Because it was never about knowing at all – it was about not being someone who has to be taught. Guided. Helped.

And being someone who never needed help was always meant to be my one useful act.

I think that's why I tend to withdraw and stay to my self – in general, really, but specifically in moments of uncertainty. I think I also have a tendency to intellectualize my thoughts and feelings to overcompensate for that, maybe? Or rather to navigate my way through that uncertainty.

I don't think it comes from a place of outright pride or arrogance about my capabilities, or to deny others the opportunity to support me, and cut off connection and collaboration, cooperation and intimacy.

I think intellectualizing has become so deeply ingrained in my inner process of sensemaking because that's what I did to fill in the gaps of simply not having a practice of outward vulnerability and emotional transparency that was modeled to me. I don't know that I often see the people in my life demonstrate that it's normal, expected, and okay to not know or to be unsure about what to think, how to feel; and how to find a way to embody that not knowing and to still find a way to move forward through that.

It was understood that the goal was to eventually arrive at solutions, the positive or bright side at the end of the tunnel. But that focus reinforced the notion that I was alone in being in the tunnel, to begin with, in not getting to the other side as quickly as everyone else – and sometimes, in the fact that I even ended up there in the first place.

* * *

Did you know with utmost certainty that this was supposed to be your journey in this life? Or did you decide for your self to prove something to someone? To prove something to your self?

I was moving out of my place – the longest I've lived anywhere other than my parents' home, about a year and a half – and realized that the reason I am avoidant to change is that allowing my life to remain stagnant allows me to become numb to the fluidity of life. It allows me to ignore my own aging, and prolong the confronting of my own mortality. Both literally, and in the sense that each stage and season of your life will look different. And in the in-between moments that connect each of those stages and seasons prompt you to mourn the previous stage and season.

I think I'm at a point where I don't want to waste my life away hoping and praying and wishing for that next moment, place, person, or thing, to the point where I am not present for my life in this current moment. I want to be more intentional about honoring each and every version of my self that helps me get closer and closer to the person I want to be and am meant to become. That requires being fully present in my process and slowing down enough to realize my growth and transformation in real time. Especially in the more challenging moments, as hard as it may be, so as to not to be in a constant rush through life looking up suddenly one day to find that who I am and how I'm experiencing the world has altered dramatically beyond recognition.

Leaving school again, and coming back home, felt like surrendering after flying too close to the Sun. It felt like an internalized form of punishment, all the things that I sought out to be, and become, I know internally rejected and avoided.

The good thing is that nothing scares me anymore. I can continue to be sad over the original, seemingly perfect thing I had hoped I could carry through to my personal finish line. But when the pressure of keeping together my own expectations throughout my journey causes me to shatter that original seemingly perfect thing; I have no choice but to realize and accept the imperfect thing. Because with the imperfect thing God and I will work together to put each piece back together and co-create an even more meaningful and perfectly honest thing.

Building a life by trying to force your self into a pair of shoes that are too big, versus being honest about who you are and where you're at and expanding your life as you grow and expand.

The difference is self-acceptance rather than thinking you're going to experience and create a life you actually enjoy when you're constantly looking at the gap between who you are and who you feel you need to become.

I'd rather think about how to live lovingly and successfully every day of my life, as opposed to thinking of success as a final destination point that I have to spend each day living half an existence until I get to it.

Journal – August 24, 2020

I'm glad I didn't forget about or abandon my self in my season of returning to my self. I needed to lose my place on the easy route to truly understand the weight of my purpose and the power and potential of my life's journey. I got to actively seek out that which brings me joy, and preview what will be my life, sooner rather than later.

I relearned my self and had to regain my identity outside of this chapter of my life. I know now that God intended for me to do and be so much more. This has simply been a stepping stone, an incubator. I am beyond grateful for my experience but there's so much more to life that I'm not even aware of yet.

However, I still have to close this chapter of my life with no loose ends. I want this semester and year to go smoothly for my self, my classmates, and my professors. We're all having to adapt and perform in a really unfortunate situation. Some of us have probably lost people, gotten sick our selves, have been out here protesting, whatever. We all deserve grace and support as we get back into the semester so everyone can succeed.

Hope used to be a form of escapism to avoid the discomfort of reality possibly being different than what I might have envisioned – being out of my control.

Moving on means giving my self permission to have hope again, and be excited about possibilities again.

Is there anything else to have hope for? Not in a negative way, but because it feels like I have arrived (at my self) and there is nowhere else to go except be here and experience this version of my self that I've worked towards being.

* * *

In the space between getting what you thought you wanted, and realizing that it wasn't what you actually needed, how do you make room for the shame of being too open to the world? For all the empty space left behind from your wanting, dreaming, and hoping?

My mind moves a lot faster than my body. Now, after catching up, I realize that I haven't been taking the kind of intentional care that I should've with my self.

I guess I'm old enough now for the impacts of my choices in life to feel real – even though I know I am supposed to have all of the time in the world, it's the first wave of fully becoming aware of my self in the world, and having to reckon with the reality of who that person is in it, and how I feel about her as a result.

I want to be better about who and how I am in my relationships in the present moment – namely my relationship with my self. I want to feel okay to surrender to the truth of my own powerlessness as much as my own limitlessness. I want to learn to appreciate how humbling that is – because it shows you that there's always so much more to experience and learn.

So much of life is about integrating Spirit, my spirit, into my lived experience and interactions with the outer world. With that, I want to go beyond just being aware of my weaknesses and inherent smallness, but to actually reconcile with that. Deeply. I guess small towns are an easy place to start.

I think it's about unlearning the compulsive need to be everywhere and everything at once versus embracing stillness, smallness, and slowness. But to also explore the world beyond what you've known and allow those experiences to inform your inner reality. To expand your perception of what's possible for your self in this life.

Notes – The Alchemist

> *"Tell your heart that the fear of suffering is worse than the suffering itself. And that no heart has ever suffered when it goes in search of its dreams, because every second of the search is a second's encounter with God and with eternity." –* The Alchemist *(pg. 134)*

My fear of suffering – of losing the illusion of stability and normalcy in my life's path – led me to confront the fact that putting my hopes and dreams into other things had me dependent on everything other than my self for validation.

I used other people, places, and things as signs from the Universe that I was on the right path, growing in the right direction. When situations didn't – and don't – go through to fruition, it's an endless gut punch back into reality (read: the story I've always told my self about my reality) that I am not actually capable or worthy of manifesting my deepest desires. My hopes and dreams go from being tangible blueprints for self-actualization to childish means of escapism.

Worse than losing progress towards the potential of who I might become on the other side of my dreams, is having to surrender to the fact that she may not ever exist at all – and that I'd have to be stuck with who and what I am at this moment.

It reminds me of the reality that I could live up to my negative potential as well: If I couldn't accomplish (or just wasn't capable of accomplishing) the one mission I did have, what is my purpose?

A lot of people say that your relationships with other people and – might I add: the institutions, places, and general world around you – mirror your internal reality and world. I believe now that leaving forced me to look inwards and find a sense of internal motivation and direction within my self.

I've also since learned that it's equally as important to give my self permission and the space to navigate grief in change and transition. Holding onto people, places, and things that, in retrospect, were placed along my life path to help me realize how I had already grown and what I was already capable of being and becoming, kept me mentally stuck rather than open and in a constant state of gratitude.

I don't know if I'll ever be in a place of complete openness to receive the goodness that life has to offer me, to make space for love and light like I wish the Universe would make space for me – with intention, care, and compassion. I don't know if I'll ever be open enough to take pride in being a diligent steward of what God has trusted me with in this lifetime: my breath, my world, my experiences, my relationships…my losses, my failures, and my lessons. For the simple fact that my heart is afraid it will have to suffer, I don't know if I'd be able to openly take on the latter parts of my journey, the suffering that is inherent to human life. I feel like it's always my fault, that there is something inherently wrong or bad

246

or flawed about me that has rendered me unworthy of life's goodness without my knowing. That no matter how many self-help books I read, therapy sessions I attend, pages of my journal I fill with my feelings, tears I cry as I force my self to feel my feelings – I am not and will never be entitled to life's goodness.

I know that I am someone who experiences and holds on to a lot of fear, which leads me avoidant and closed off to what my life and the world have to offer right in front of me. I am constantly looking to something or somewhere else for escape or solace or hope. However I ended up here. That is where I'm at.

I'm afraid that by moving on and allowing my self to be and become more than where I am right now that means I don't love my past or even present selves. I have to let go of her to give my future self a chance to exist, let alone be great.

Journal – June 30, 2021

I've been putting my happiness in the prospect of things coming through in the future. That means I'm not happy now, and I put a lot of pressure and power into the future. As opposed to investing faith in power into what I have in the present. As opposed to believing that my journey will come through for me in the future.

I'm able to "struggle" because I am confident that there will be a reward at the end. But then when the reward doesn't come immediately, it feels like "What was all the struggle actually for?" It feels like then I wasted all my time, at that point the struggle wasn't worth it.

I don't know if that means that I have to move as though I may not get the things that I want and that is integrity and faithfulness. Black women have been taught – people have been taught – that struggle breeds reward or even that struggle is its own reward.

Maybe shifting to a paradigm of not delaying happiness or abundance but prioritizing my journey to be abundant, joyful, and peaceful now; because the reward may never come. I can still grow and be challenged but the constant struggling and depriving my self and denying my self of joy in this moment is no longer worth it.

* * *

What's holding you back from abundance? Specifically, from finding abundance right where you are and within your self?

After a lifetime of longing and waiting to get to that next moment..that next place – how do you learn to sit squarely in the space between dreaming and grieving? To be in all the places you find your self without resistance?

There's often a split between being and becoming – this is where conflict happens.

There's a need you feel to push your own agenda or plan instead of listening to God and your own inner voice for guidance on what to do. Or, more importantly, when to just be.

248

I would feel as though other people or entities having to constantly teach me or give me feedback or critique reinforces my deeply rooted belief that I'm not smart or capable enough to figure things out on my own. I have felt like I've been in a limbo stage of constant paternalization, where life tells me "You'll figure things out when you're older," and the feeling left out of some magic key to life that everyone seems to have but me.

This leads me to feel like I had to work extra hard to figure out problems on my own. It eventually became such a subconscious process, that trying to unlearn it to ask for support, open my self up to connection and collaboration, and stand in vulnerability and healthy conflict, all felt deeply uncomfortable and signaled to my nervous system to get out of the triggering situation, quickly. This led to a lot of the same self-sabotaging behaviors of avoidance and passivity that I was working to unlearn in the first place.

What does it mean to create mental and emotional space to actually be present and connect – with your self, your life, with others – rather than remain hypervigilant for things that resonate with who you think you are and are becoming?

I see that your hurt is in "Why me?" or in this case, "Why not me?"

You feel like you could learn something from the answer, or at least be able to move forward. But try not to stay there too long. There are other places to go and other things to do.

That kind of suffering comes from the resistance of thinking you shouldn't feel that way – that you shouldn't be seeking that kind of external validation anyways.

But you're really looking for a mirror to reflect back qualities you want to see in and experience for your self.

There's also suffering in wanting and waiting – for other people to see your hurt and disappointment. But I believe that's another opportunity to instead redirect your gaze inward to see and validate your self and your own experiences. It's real and valid because I am living it, not because of how someone perceived and defined it externally.

I think this could allow you to just sit where you are and reconnect with who and where you are.

Being a "good" or successful person doesn't stop bad or unexpected things from happening. You have to deal with the deeper sense of deficiency and threat towards whatever false sense of security you have.

You felt like that mentality gave you drive and ambition, when really it enables you to disregard your human needs in the present moment and the reality of your fallibility in comparison to the Universe and its power.

Even though it may be difficult, it will help you expand your capacity and confidence to fully embrace the present moment. The goal is to work directly with the underlying identity when it is activated, rather than just moving through it. This will help you relax in triggering situations.

What inner conflicts are obscuring these deeper capacities?

- *I am struggling to accept that life can be the compounding or exponentiating of my mistakes.*
- *Maybe I can try again next lifetime?*
- *I believed that aimlessness left me vulnerable. When I knew where I was going, I felt fine – confident even. As soon as I hit a roadblock or a wrong turn that facade dropped immediately.*
- *"Fair weather friend" – I think my confidence and self-assurance are genuine until I have a legitimate reason to not be (roadblock, lack of clarity, or detour) but I do not need to force not knowing or confusion or being a damsel in distress— I know. I can say that in this present moment, I need guidance and clarity to either reassure or redirect my previous conclusions.*

By giving your self permission to be more intentional yet more open-handed towards the Universe – you give your self room to offer more genuine and powerful yeses to life. To what you truly want to do and that truly speaks to you, versus what you feel you need to do out of obligation.

For the sake of just taking up space and enjoying your self in this life incarnation – allow space for the inner parts of you that make you you, *to actualize your human potential in this lifetime.*

What would it feel like to be full of your self? To fully take up space and just be exactly where you are?

It's okay to want to just take up space by just being. You don't have to earn the right to take up space or earn the space itself. Taking up space can be light and life-giving. It doesn't have to be weighed down or drained by responsibility.

You need to take up space unapologetically to feel and express good emotions like power, joy, pleasure, and excitement about what you're saying yes to. To be clear on when what you're saying yes to may cause ego inflation or when it might be indicative of disingenuous motives.

It's okay to give your self space to examine that the ways you've operated can be self-limiting. It is okay to acknowledge and reckon with the fact that this idealized version of your self failed or, in subtle ways, was not able to live up to your own high expectations.

It seems as though you've internalized so much of self-development messaging that is rooted in teaching you to hate your past self – even though they got you to where you are today. You could probably learn something from every version of who they were and how they showed up in the world.

But know that you have to let it go in order to make room for a higher version of your self. And approach that compassionately and with gratitude for how far that version of your self got you.

Notes – undated

"Hold space for, be present with, and witness. They are all forms of respect."

Make space and guard it fiercely

You are home, where you can be rooted

Ground your self and your dreams in reality

Embody personal presence in your own unique way – wisdom, great clarity, compassion, patience, strength, or generosity; power, love, flexibility, confidence, or trust

- *not as much about your identity, unique qualities, lived experience, dreams, and accomplishments, etc.*
- *still embodying those aspects of you – individuation is more about clarifying those aspects of you to be a more transparent vessel*
- *Showing up as the most authentic version of you, not as the end, but as the vessel/vehicle to your true self*

Impersonal presence = agape love for all people

Personal presence = love as this unique expression of me, loving a unique expression of someone else

Journeying from a place of lack and longing versus from a place of openness and gratitude for what has been, what is, and what could be

To be held, seen, and cared for fully and wholly

To be and experience a steady love and constant presence

Until now, comfort, stability, and safety always felt borrowed. I want to know what it means to cultivate it

for myself over time and experience it, live in it...rest in it. Embody it.

"Wherever you go, there you are." I am someone who might be critically bored with her life and who grew to need the illusion of movement and possibility to feel like I am real and meaningful and capable and to be assured that the space I occupy in the world is not in vain.

How do you hold space between your need for presence, peace, and joy, and a sincere/genuine desire to make the most out of your numbered days?

"If something isn't growing, it's dead." The time – my time – will pass anyways. How do I find balance between being and becoming? How do I live in a way that demonstrates the value of my existence without needing to find a way to maximize every single second to the point of not fully living at all?

I am frustrated with the fact that I am not there yet. That I don't know yet. That I have not become yet. I am much closer than I was, but the funny thing about growing up is that when you get through your "I know everything about life" phase – you realize that you actually know nothing, and it is equal parts terrifying and humbling.

What would it feel like to abandon your incessant need to live mentally in the future – by temporarily releasing all hopes and dreams altogether? What would it feel like to just be here? Firmly and fully.

It's one thing to release your hopes for the future temporarily as to afford your self a moment of peace and mindfulness. It's another thing to have to abandon them because your immovable grip on your dreams has created a cage that keeps you from ever experiencing that peace.

Because the Hope and North Star were just to keep you going. It wasn't necessarily meant to be the main thing.

I invite you to see beyond the idea that the purpose of life is always made to be about the journey ahead – your potential and the trajectory of your life. What if it could be more about finding a home within your self and then approaching your life's journey from a place of security and enoughness; gratitude and curiosity?

I invite you to try getting deeply acquainted with your self and your life in the present moment because, really, that's all you have.

I'm in a period of just expanding to just be aware of all the shitty parts that I've tried really hard to hide or avoid. To just notice them in real-time and just be aware of them and accept them. To acknowledge my fear of my ability to claim my stake in the world and make something meaningful out of it.

I invite you to cultivate an appreciation for the difficult work of being emotionally present for your life. To prioritize the deeply personal work of deciding who and how you want to be in the world, and how you want to approach the practice of living. But also making time to just enjoy life as well not be so bogged down by that work because it's heavy, regardless of how you slice it.

I'm realizing that actually living it and being present for your actual life, rather than just for the idea of your life, are two different things – the former requiring much more energy and attention. It can be a lot, so my focus is to just allow the journey to unfold and recognize the work I have put in this far, and spend more time holding space for self-care and quality life experiences to make the journey sustainable.

I feel like I previously have been hesitant to integrate the two because, at the end of the day, my relationship with my self in my inner world is the most intimate one that I have. There's a feeling of not wanting to share that with others. There's a feeling of "you all can have the reserved impassive me."

I wouldn't say one or the other is my better self, but I think the version of my self that was more willing and ready to take risks in life has not been given a chance to really navigate the world – which is what creates that power imbalance. But what I really have needed to learn and understand, is that the version of my self now – that is more in tune with her intuition, who is slower to act – also holds a lot of wisdom. She isn't reckless, she isn't the type to just move on a whim. She thinks before she acts. She is intentional.

Notes – The Sovereignty of Quiet

"Bonner's final characterization disturbs all of the ways that waiting and interiority get rendered as merely domestic, or feminine, or enfeebled. Instead waiting

is without limit and is truly cosmopolitan. It is also important that the essay does not end in triumph, as if the reader or narrator has overcome the exterior world. No, since this articulation of the interior is quiet, it ends in possibility rather than achievement. There is no triumph to be had, especially since the self is not calibrated against an external measurement. There is just the work of being complicatedly human. And in this work, the compass for subjectivity is the interior...For the narrator, there is no other measure but her self, for as flawed as this might be, it is a better compass than to give in to what is exterior. She, this person who is black and female, measures her self by her self, by her capacity for quiet; she surrenders to her interior as a location of agency." – The Sovereignty of Quiet (*pg. 44-45*)

I believe there is a higher power – God – and the Universe – the forces of nature, and the ripple effect of other people's free will – that are beyond my understanding and control. There are things I will have to respond to – and how I choose to respond to what crosses my path *is* within my control. I can't do anything about anything else.

What if you never find answers to those questions? Will you still allow your self to experience some other form of fulfillment, actualization, meaning, and clarity about who you are and why you're here?

This used to cause me anxiety because of the discomfort and focusing so much on the future and not being easy on my self now that I no longer know how or where to direct my energetic, emotional, mental, and physical aims.

I think I am afraid of life/God/the Universe dealing decisive and final cards while I'm still trying to figure out which cards are in my hand.

Maybe it's a sign that I don't trust life to deliver my lessons to me in the order and manner in which I'm meant to have them. Maybe I need to work towards making peace with the things I am still subconsciously toiling over and give my self permission to not feel like I have to figure out all the things today.

My first thought is never to ask God for guidance, support, or answers in general. My first instinct is never to lean on another person when I'm unable to do something my self. My instinct is to suffer, struggle and strain in silence, finesse my way to achieve my desired outcome. Through my walk with Christ, I've learned how easy it is to just say God, I need your help right now. How relieving it is to know within the depths of my soul that no weapon formed against me shall prosper and that They have already gone before me to see me through this life.

The point is not whether or not I can accomplish the goal my self. The point is that I don't experience life as fully if I don't allow my self to collaborate with others, share my life with others, or let other people see me through the full spectrum of my best and worst moments. It's the more acceptable manifestation of "control freak," I think, when I don't want others to worry about me, go out of their way for me, or see me at my literal worst.

The point is not whether or not I can open the jar by my self, because if I try at first and don't succeed, I'll keep trying and straining until I get it. The point is that when I ask someone else to open the jar for me, I indirectly say I trust you enough to ask you to help me with this. When I choose to discuss something that I'm struggling with emotionally with a friend, I indirectly say I trust you enough to share my inner world with you. The fine print of that already indirect statement reads Please be careful with it. And when they are, it affirms that this person is safe and that I can continue to trust them and cultivate emotional safety with them over time. When they aren't – the experiences throughout my life that stay with me a little longer than the former – I become apprehensive, almost like a puppy scarred from negative reinforcement. I walk on eggshells a little more cautiously and tie my mask on a little more tightly. It registers in the most fundamental parts of my being that authenticity in this space is not safe.

The energy required to maintain this philosophy as a way of life is energy I no longer have. To go through life not solidified and confident in who you are is not the way I want to live my life. I want to trust people. I want to loosen the child's grip I want to have over every part of my life. I want to let someone else open the jar for me. I want to feel confident that if I open my self up to what this world has to offer, I won't be let down, hurt, or permanently wounded.

That thought turns me back to the opening scripture of this

259

chapter, Psalms 16:3. "Commit to the Lord whatever you do, and your plans will be established." God wants us to feel the joy of our plans coming to fruition. They want to see our plans through to fruition. It's when we don't trust God enough to make it happen, we take the matters of our life into our own hands and keep hold with a vice grip. We suffer, struggle, and strain to see our plans through, and when we (inevitably) meet the point where we can't find the strength to make the final push over the finish line, we suffer, struggle, and strain some more.

Another thing I like about this verse is that it lets me know that I do not have to do this alone. While society loves to ingrain in us the principles of individualism, which for some of us can be a perfectly fine way to achieve success, there's no way that I – in all of my flawed human existence – can actualize my dreams (including those currently unbeknownst to me) all on my own. Even if I choose to enlist the help of other people, similarly flawed in their human existence, that will only take me but so far. Other people cannot help me become the person God has called me to be, only They can do that. They can be great supporters and confidants, strengthen my network, and keep me sane in the pursuit of what's mine, but they cannot "establish" my plans for me.

A false sense of purpose that you constructed and decided and asserted into the world, versus a co-collaboration between you and the Universe based on what the world needs and your unique being and offerings. It's fine to have dreams but leave enough room for God to use you in the way They want to use you.

I don't want to fight in order to be seen and heard (by other people...or by God). But does that automatically mean that I trust my self to be in tune with God and the Universe? To trust and have faith?

It's not about the destination itself – it's more about faith, and where you place it, in whom you place it. You can put it in other people, your achievements, status, etc. Ultimately, you need to work to see your self as being worthy of having faith put in you. To put your faith in God and in your own divinity.

In order to show up fully and authentically, you have to allow that part of you to be witnessed, too.

I feel like I *should* be someone who has hope... who is hopeful. Someone who believes in the positive and who is not just always waiting for the negative – believing that everything is inevitably negative, waiting for the proverbial shoe to drop. I guess I wouldn't know that either way. It just is.

I believe I was orienting my dreams around short-sighted aims. And I can acknowledge that there are a lot of things I wasn't able to achieve for my younger self, and a lot of promises I feel I wasn't able to keep.

I do want to acknowledge the grief, regret, and heartbreak that I do feel and that has happened, but I know that I also do not want to stay there. I will admit that it is hard to remember that option is available without first losing sight of the fact that while, yes – that is still a part of me and my story, I am in a different place.

She spent so many of her days not feeling seen and heard, wishing and waiting for the day she'd get to finally make her mark in a place where things were happening. I feel like I have spent a lot of my time trying to prove these inherent limits wrong. It feels like fully moving forward would mean I'm abandoning and forgetting about that version of my self.

I think I am struggling with the fear that I am not or was not ever capable of following through on those dreams and promises, and with the idea that what I wanted was never meant for me and that I wasted my energy and limited time.

I want to give my self permission to move forward. To know that it's okay to accept redirection, and to change your mind. To know that you are not held hostage to any iteration of who you previously were and what you previously wanted.

There are things that you knew and things that you've learned. You couldn't (and can't) predict the future, how could you expect that of your self?

The disconnect between my future self and past self is wide: past me has done her job, and future me has her own problems to worry about. All I can do is my personal best to take care of my self in the present.

The desire to grow and evolve feels like an act of self-betrayal but I know that allowing my self to remain stagnant is also, self-betrayal.

There's a feeling of grief in remembering that I cannot at least attempt to remove the burdens of my past selves. However, I'm thankful to her — every version of her — because she held us down and continued to show up for her self and for me in order to try to make sense of this complex mess that is our future.

Journal – September 15, 2020

I don't believe any one person has been with me through the trenches of my personal journey and growth. That isn't inherently a bad thing, but it becomes difficult when it comes to integrating what I've learned by having done all this internal work on my self – with new realizations, a newfound sense of self-confidence, and new perspectives. Trying to integrate my self into a world that is largely the same. You don't know how to hold your new self up against old fires, so it engulfs you yet again – but maybe this time a little less completely. Or, better yet, you're able to move more quickly to rebuild your self from those newfound ashes. The goal is to only get a slight burn, or maybe a little hot, but ultimately resist the flame entirely.

Where do you go – who do you look to – to remember your truth?

Before getting into who I might have the opportunity to become in the future, I want to be at peace with the person I am now. I want to learn to value and gain a deeper understanding of who she is and what she hopes for, who she is becoming, and what she is building. I want to get better at appreciating how she expresses her higher self and God's voice with and through her voice in the present moment.

Even more so, there is a part of me that wants to get more acquainted and familiar with – to learn how to hold more compassion for – all that I am not, and may never become.

Where do you aspire to go and who do you aspire to be if what you were previously journeying towards no longer feels worth pursuing?

You know to first seek clarity and alignment with your highest self, to be a co-creator with God and with the Universe, rather than trying to take control all on your own…regardless of where that takes you. You know that all you can do is hope to get there with your heart and soul intact.

It's one thing to dream about infinite versions of your self – all of the lives you might be able to live and experience. It's another to live the one life that you have and be decisive about the choices you make in favor of the person you become. To trust your self or life or God or the Universe enough to just follow your path and not question it.

If my life had worked out the way I'd wanted it to, maybe I'd continue to be the person who lived a life of checked boxes. The person who lived out their "ancestors' wildest dreams" rather than interrogating whether it actually aligned with their own.

The expectation of living up to your own self-directed positive potential is just a lot. In some moments, I want to be allowed to just be. To be able to give my self permission to just be. But I accept and appreciate the challenge of having to be still and firmly present for my life. To be an active participant in my life and its outcomes.

I'm still afraid that I won't experience the depths of the beauty that life has to offer. I'm sure I'll scratch the surface and check the box of having lived a good life, but I don't know that my soul is open to receiving the highs because it's so afraid of the lows.

What if I just allowed my self to be exactly where I'm at — to feel sad about what I've lost — without forcing my self to focus my gaze on what might be ahead?

I'm practicing what it means to believe deeply that I'm both inherently deserving of everything I desire and also more than okay not to be pressed to receive all the things at the same time.

I have had to acknowledge my own part and my suffering by thinking that life and all of its goodness would pass me by if I didn't accept it right as I decided I wanted it, or when it seemed available to me. I'm learning what it means to deeply trust and believe – and demonstrate my belief – that what is for me will not pass me.

What does it mean to see and acknowledge and hold the things you most sincerely long for, and – not outright reject them before they reject you but – to let them go with love? To not be recognized and rewarded by that which you have pedestalized? To give up your previously helped beliefs about success and failure? To entertain the possibility of not being chosen by that which you pedestalized and releasing your self from your attachment to your feelings about what already is?

Journal – October 2020

I am learning how to take up space in the world without influence or imposition.

I have a more stable relationship and a higher level of comfort with my interior world and my emotions. Therapy is helping me to better exist in and navigate the world and take up space fully as my highest self. To achieve a level of self-acceptance that allows me to be in the world as I imagine and dream of my self and my life.

I think I finally understand and am reckoning with what it means, for me, to be a Black woman in this world – necessary and needed yet unprotected.

That's my gravity. It just is.

Gravity pulls you in different directions – more heavily weighted by your own shame. Other people's perceptions and definitions of you matter more than your own understanding of your self – so why fight against gravity?

And I think there are parts of me that are still longing for validation from the arbiters of gravity that I am good and whole and on the way there. Wherever there ends up being.

The past is the past, and there's nothing that I can do about that. I am able to sit with that in a way that is relieving because it is done and written. Still, I think the future feels scary and abstract and out of my control. But I also feel that I can't go back to passively waiting for the future to arrive because I've seen what can happen when I put forth an intentional effort toward alchemy.

It's not to say that you can't show up and be big too, that you can't have big dreams. I think it's just about grounding your dreams and reality and accepting the heaviness that comes with gravity.

I'm no longer carrying gravity with a feeling of shame. With or without my effort, it just is. And I don't want to lose my self in a losing fight against what just is.

I've spent a lot of time projecting my perception of life and the world onto other people – because I was subconsciously looking for my review to be validated and affirmed. Whole time, especially as that inner voice became stronger – this made my internal critique towards my self and others stronger. It was all the information and affirmation I needed.

I think that the world does not show us what it means to have confidence, or how to heal and build our confidence. The world does not offer grace for lack of confidence that is a result of the myriad ways our confidence is destroyed.

I don't believe that I'm unhappy with my self or my life for acknowledging that fact. The younger version of me might've been a daydreamer, but she was able to use that to evoke a feeling of more self embodiment and conviction, and confidence within her self right where she was.

Maybe there is a part of me that is just disappointed – namely with my self – about that. Maybe I subconsciously believe that being disappointed is a result of me not being worthy or valuable. But disappointment just is. It's a part of life.

I don't think that you are wholly and fundamentally disappointed with your life. With your self. I think there has been an accumulation of many small and large disappointments that have stayed with you for longer than they should've. I think you believe that if you move on from these many disappointments, you are somehow affirming to your self – the way everyone else affirms to you – that your disappointment doesn't matter.

I think that to grapple with these many disappointments, you realized that all that you really have control over is your self. And you realize that maybe it was easier to focus on erasing that within your self that might've led to your disappointment.

I think I've historically felt very helpless and naive when it came to talking about my personal difficulty with disappointment. I think I also don't seek support in those moments now because I feel like, "No I want to do it my self and I need the space and time to figure it out."

I guess there's a difference between that and still understanding that some things in life are sometimes just my responsibility to figure out for my self, and that I do need to give my self the space and time to do that of my own volition and in my own time, but that I can still allow other people to support me while I do that deeply personal work.

But I don't think there's anything else to do. The only thing that I have the energy for right now is to just sit in the disappointment. Not forever, but just long enough to fully be in it to know that even though it's uncomfortable, it's okay.

Your life is still worth living and being fully in despite all your disappointment. I don't want to make you feel like you have to try to see the positive or the learning experience out of your deep disappointment and discomfort. Just be in it and allow it to suck and know that there will be a time when you won't feel that way anymore.

I think the space you have been trying to figure out how to take up will come when you acknowledge your disappointment. When you allow your self to sit and be in that feeling you'll realize that it is then easier to face the world in an honest way.

You are not ungrateful, you are not a bad person, and you're not unfaithful when you acknowledge disappointment. When you are honest about the reality of what it has meant to relate to your self and to others throughout your life. So – how will you decide to grapple with all your disappointment?

* * *

What does it mean to feel at home with your self or to find a home within your self?

Since I was a kid, as I grew in my awareness (and at some point frustration) that my world sometimes seemed too small for me, I longed for the chance to take up space in the world, to explore and interact, to learn and discover. I sometimes dreamt about what it would be like to move to a noisy, more lively city –to a place where things are happening; where life feels like it's moving forward and gives way for meaningful progress.

I assumed that actualizing your higher self meant, taking who you know your self to be in your experience within your inner world in forcing that upon the outer world, I realize now that when you surrender to the fact that there's so much more to all of this then you realize you're able to see that it's not about you. But not in a way that makes you feel like you don't matter at all, but rather in a way that allows you to see the ripple effects of how who you are and how you show up impacts the world around you and to accept that the world — for better or worse — has impacted you. That you are not exempt from the implications of the world that we live in that by accepting your positioning in it, you can better understand how to effectively transform your self and your small corner of the world.

In my small corner of the world – starting in my hometown – it's quiet here…never too much going on. I think that because of that fact, maybe I get anxious about potentially getting lost in people, places, and things that are not (able to be) grounded or still or quiet themselves. And I don't know that I've understood how to articulate that again in the midst of so much movement and things happening just in life and in the world.

As I've grown in my understanding of how that fear of engulfment of all this outside energy has impacted me moving into a space of learning what does it mean to set boundaries so that I'm able to show up and have the energy and the emotional space and the emotional reserves to be open and vulnerable and more in my body and more in tune with my emotions to express them and actually be vulnerable in the moment as opposed to intellectualizing them?

I know that I deeply need the freedom to explore and to remember that I have options to be able to feel that in my bones. But, ultimately, I do value the stability and security I grew up with here and that I know also lives in my bones. Not so much complacency and stagnation, but to know that I have a place to be rooted and grounded and anchored. I know that I have a home.

I've also since learned that it's not always about the outward work, but about redirecting your energy to do the inner work so that you can be more open and receptive to how God wants to make space for you in the world.

I used to think my journey until this point was solely about seeking belonging – but as some outward locus of control – to alleviate the feeling of your own being feeling foreign. I now believe it's simply finding a balance of connectedness and separateness – to acknowledge and accept the people, places, and experiences that made you, without over-identifying with where you come from or where you're going. To be able to more easily remember that all I have, all I have ever had, is who and where I am in this present moment.

I've spent much of my life looking to external sources to feel like I mattered. I believed I didn't matter, and I was biased toward people and situations that affirmed that belief.

There's an idea of what once was or what could be that is represented by this place. I don't know whether to reject it or embrace it.

If I reject it, maybe that really means I'm rejecting the part of my self that it represents. My fears, my limitations…all the things I hate most about my self.

If I embrace it, does that mean I'm vulnerable to the possibility of my fears being realized? For the possibility that what I desire most won't ultimately want me back?

Either way, maybe I'm avoiding another possibility: the truth being revealed to me so that I can make a choice and move forward.

I don't know if either of the former possibilities are for better or worse. I just know that when I refocus my lens on what is most important – me and how I feel, what I want – that is not only being disregarded but devalued in the face of all the other voices in my head and around me putting pressure and urgency on your decisions and their outcomes.

I feel like I've had to get comfortable with an inherent level of separateness and aloneness.

Well, I do desire to be more deeply connected to the people around me and the world more broadly. Now I think that what I really wanted for my self in this life so far is agency. Not simply to be physically alone, but to know and find comfort in the fact that that solitude is mine. To be able to exist in and experience the world for my self, without having to carry and filter through energies and voices that are not mine.

I don't think anybody comes into this life, inherently, or immediately expecting the worst from it. I think we internalize the messages from our personal experiences, or from what we see in the world around us that either we or people who share our same identities or experiences are constantly disappointed and let down.

We look to someone or something for some hope of a happy ending, to maybe reground us, in some sense of the possibility of goodness finding its way to us too.

I don't wanna say that I don't care anymore but I know that either way I am secure in the fact that I am good where I'm at with what I have.

It's not because I feel like I don't deserve goodness, and I don't even think that is because I don't know what I want. Sometimes I just feel like what I want might just be too much and that is not possible – either at all or just for me.

The space and time embodiment required for deeper emotional connection – to see and be seen and acknowledged in a meaningful way – just doesn't feel possible in a world where everyone is focused on the next thing and the next thing on acquiring more and more people, accomplishments, money, etc.

Maybe the hope lies in the opportunity we have each day to create space in and for your self to reconnect with your self and heal and clear out what is distracting and weighing you down and allow room for goodness to find you.

What is keeping you here? I don't know that it is or has to be some grand or significant reason. This is just where I'm at but I also know that this is not all that there is. That I am not a tree and that I can in fact move.

But if you take a moment to be still and listen, what is Spirit trying to tell you? Are you even listening? Do you even know what They sound like?

In that space, there is everything and nothing. All the chaos and catastrophe that feels inevitable, all the possibilities and abundance that is available – and the stillness that also exists in that ether.

If you allow enough time to pass, you at some point begin to hear nature, the movement of all the other beings in the Universe happening around you. You allowed room for synchronicities to finally take their mark. Room, and space, for you to actually notice.

While it may feel like the world is mirroring back unnecessary fear, worry, judgment, etc. – being so focused on external sources of truth will disorient you. No one can tell you what your core motivation – what your truth – is.

It's not about other people or the world, as big as they seem. It's about what your thoughts and feelings about others may suggest about your own perception of your self, and about how deeply you're able to hold your self with empathy, understanding, and compassion.

You're trying to treat a mirror as a window to look at what you think you perceive in other people's lives and to compare your self. To view your worthiness through other peoples' actions and journeys. Whole time you're subconsciously avoiding your reflection and the information and wisdom it could be sharing with you.

Think of it like this: The only thing that matters is where your thoughts about your self came from. Interrogating that matters.

It's your world and everyone else is just living in it. Not in a self-centered way but in that everyone around you and all of your experiences are mirrors.

I feel like I've had to get comfortable with an inherent level of separateness and aloneness.

Well, I do desire to be more deeply connected to the people around me and the world more broadly. Now I think that what I really wanted for my self in this life so far is agency. Not simply to be physically alone, but to know and find comfort in the fact that that solitude is mine. To be able to exist in and experience the world for my self, without having to carry and filter through energies and voices that are not mine.

I don't think anybody comes into this life, inherently, or immediately expecting the worst from it. I think we internalize the messages from our personal experiences, or from what we see in the world around us that either we or people who share our same identities or experiences are constantly disappointed and let down.

We look to someone or something for some hope of a happy ending, to maybe reground us, in some sense of the possibility of goodness finding its way to us too.

I don't wanna say that I don't care anymore but I know that either way I am secure in the fact that I am good where I'm at with what I have.

It's not because I feel like I don't deserve goodness, and I don't even think that is because I don't know what I want. Sometimes I just feel like what I want might just be too much and that is not possible – either at all or just for me.

The space and time embodiment required for deeper emotional connection – to see and be seen and acknowledged in a meaningful way – just doesn't feel possible in a world where everyone is focused on the next thing and the next thing on acquiring more and more people, accomplishments, money, etc.

Maybe the hope lies in the opportunity I have each day to

create space in and for my self to recenter and heal and clear out what is distracting and weighing me down and allow room for goodness to find me.

What is keeping you here? I don't know that it is or has to be some grand or significant reason. This is just where I'm at but I also know that this is not all that there is. That I am not a tree and that I can in fact move.

You have the opportunity to reframe your self-perception – to give your self permission to see and do and be more, if that's what you want.

I want to develop an ability to get very quiet and listen to what Spirit is telling me. To intentionally fight for that space, rather than wait passively for life to create that space for me, or to avoid it altogether.

To recognize that I have the opportunity to be the person who is coming and/or going, and at other times, you have the opportunity to be the person who sits and waits, listens and receives. Because neither is inherently bad, there is simply a time for one or the other.

I want to know what it means to create space to really understand my self and the people, places, and experiences that made me without feeling like my answers and solutions are out there somewhere else.

And I know that I don't want my relationship with everything that informed my self-perception – my home, my upbringing, my experiences – to become another entity to which I outsource my power and self-worth. But I also know that I don't want to move through my life believing that they don't matter, either.

I was made in Their image, as were all of the things that made me. So there's some level of divinity that is within me and embodied through me that deserves to be acknowledged, respected, and held with compassion.

And by not treating my self with love, kindness, and respect, what does that say about who and what made me?

This shift in perspective invites me to better honor the space I take up in the world, yet surrender to the fact that there are entities and elements, nature and circumstances and people, that exist outside of me, that existed before me, and that will exist after I am gone.

Instead of seeing Them as another external entity whom I have to please and get validation from, I now aim to see my self as an extension or vessel of Them. How can I look within my (highest) self for balance, alignment, and wisdom?

The beauty of holiness and security in your self is that you can just be in tune with who and what you are. You don't necessarily need to look around at the world and see the things you want to do reflected in front of you. Sometimes it being on your heart and mind is enough confirmation.

The true possibility doesn't necessarily exist solely in the future, but in the present moment where you can stand firmly in the extent of your power to own your agency and self-actualize.

I can trust my inner knowing that there is always something to hope for, and that my only prayer is that God covers me and the Earth keeps me as I continue to make the journey there.

I feel like so much of my life up until this point has been like growing into a pair of shoes that always seemed too big for me. Trying to be and become something or someone whose essence was way over my head. Trying to force Main Character Energy in such a small town.

I know now that while that feeling is absolutely valid, it does not have to be my sole truth or the lens through which I see the world and live my life: What are the stories I tell my self about who I am, where I come from, where I've been and what I've experienced?

It's not about invalidating those stories – and the thoughts and feelings associated with them. It's about reframing them, giving my self an opportunity to view everything from an equally valid yet more empowering vantage point.

Because – in reality, I was always on my way to becoming the exact person I was meant to be. I now have the opportunity to break those same shoes in and experience them in the world with more comfort and wiggle room.

The version of my self that used to find safety and comfort

in predictability has evolved – things that felt familiar now seem foreign, and I now find that comfort in my self before anything or anyone else.

Maybe the idea of staying in one place or fixating on one thing to save you created a lot of fear about whether you'd end up stagnant and not fully living up to your life's potential, but I think it can also show you how much can be moved around you and within you.

I don't have a problem with who I am or where I come from at all, I think I fear losing all of the things that made me, how they look and feel in their current state. To sit with the grief caused by moving on and moving forward through life.

I now believe that it's about accepting that you are, in fact, of the world and that you have the *power* to hold on to the parts of it that resonate with you and to work to unlearn what doesn't. I also know that even if the world I'm building for my self crumbled from underneath my feet – I know I always have a home to return to.

Storyteller. Dream Weaver. Wise Woman.

"I tell my students, 'When you get these jobs that you have been so brilliantly trained for, just remember that your real job is that if you are free, you need to free somebody else. If you have some power, then your job is to empower somebody else." – *Toni Morrison,* O, The Oprah Magazine (*2003*)

"I believe there is power in words, power in asserting our existence, our experience, our lives, through words." – *Jesmyn Ward,* The Fire This Time: A New Generation Speaks About Race (2016)

I **understand why people settle now.**

Being an active participant in your life is intensive in that you actively have to decide to reinforce what you know to be true or choose differently than what you've always known.

It takes work to find a balance between living life fully engaged and on purpose, and checking things off the proverbial checklist. To build and manage a life versus flowing through the art of simply being alive and resting in the blessing of feeling life in your body.

It's – not necessarily easier – but a more worthwhile use of your limited time on Earth, to pursue joy and happiness, love, connection, and fulfillment rather than a singular vision of exceptionality in all areas of your life that may or may not come to pass when it's all said and done.

I am learning to get deeply comfortable with the tension between grieving and welcoming new beginnings. Moment to moment, season to season.

Instead of deep pain, struggle, and discomfort – I'm trying to do better at recognizing and inviting in deep joy, love, care, and inspiration. I want to be better at inviting in connection to something higher than my self.

Younger me was smart, she had the information, but she wasn't wise. She hadn't yet gotten the experience to have embodied knowing, just surface-level knowing.

There comes a point when you have to make clear decisions and stand on your wants, needs, values, and dreams to choose your life and make choices about your life. This, rather than dreaming about it, thinking, reflecting.

When those assumptions and perspectives are truly challenged – how do you respond? And what does the potential discrepancy say about you?

* * *

Writing these essays has been an opportunity to confront: how deeply I have not felt truly seen and known throughout my life. How much I don't think I have truly been able to see and know my self.

I've had to confront how much of my self I have denied my self and others access to. I've offered a very flattened version of my self – absolving my self of the full range of my emotions, to subconsciously punish my self for not being enough? Maybe because there's a part of me that doesn't trust my self to reach all of my hopes and dreams on my own?

It's been an opportunity to unlearn an ego-driven victim mindset: As I have grown to be someone who avoids being seen and known because it is so unfamiliar to me, I'm learning to reframe that towards a posture of responsibility to face my self and address my stuff to heal. To experience my self as whole, first, and to also be available to others so that I can do my work and be of service without resentment.

I discover, articulate, and assert my freedom in what I write and create. And I believe there is power in searching for language, and clarity to better understand your self and your experiences for your self. And then to use that language as a bridge or an offering for connection with others.

283

Using language and writing to navigate through life to the best of my ability at that moment – not about having everything figured out, but about constantly being in conversation (with my self, God, and others) about what direction my life is headed in and how I'm thinking critically about that, being intentional about that. Or – about how I'm allowing space for spontaneity and happenstance, for living and being and allowing.

Unfortunately, I am a writer so it does often have to happen for the whole world to see. That's just a part of my process of connecting and offering something for other people to connect with and see themselves in. Making sure to document it all as I'm living, creating, building.

I want to write and complete the project and get it out of the way, move on from this chapter of my life so that I can live. Make room for new dreams and projects. To allow my self to move beyond working in solitude to collaborating and creating spaces for people to experience the same creative and intellectual agency that I have created for my self. To see what else there is to the experience of being human.

Writing has been a tool to affirm my thoughts and ideas that I have about my self and life and the world. To write the way to healing, into a better future for my self and hopefully for others.

The best writing advice I've ever gotten was to *live:* I'm so much more than a writer – I'm a visionary and dream weaver. And what I really want is connection. I now view writing as a more passive means to connect by documenting my journey toward the most authentic version of my self. By allowing my writing to be the place where I cannot perform.

It's been a way to make sense of it and make meaning of my experiences, but at the end of the day, there's still a book to write.

You have to be definitive and put something on paper, you can't just sit and think about what you would say, about how the story will eventually come together from beginning to end, about what you will have written and how people will react. In living and writing you have to make decisions down to each paragraph, sentence, and word.

Sort out the irrational and rational thoughts, work to change self-defeating thoughts, emotions, and beliefs; and replace them with a functional outlook, emotional regulation, and constructive actions.

It feels like I have gleaned all the lessons, so what is the point of continuing to sit with them and keep my self stuck in the past?

I think that I have lived the contents of this book. And now in writing the contents of this book, it is an opportunity to demonstrate that I value my self in my life in my story. It's an opportunity to think through not just how to get through the hardships or the challenges or the moments in my life that felt very unclear and the feeling that that lack of clarity was insurmountable.

I'm now able to see the smallness and the limitlessness of my humanity at the same time. I'm able to look back on those experiences with a pearl of casual wisdom and self-accountability, because I know that I figured it out in the end. I'm able to give my self the space to get what I need to get off my chest because I know that I need it – but I also know not to let my self stay there too long because I know there is more for us ahead.

My stories aren't valid because they're universal truths. They're valid because they are my experiences. It would be nice to be able to speak to larger social issues and movements, but don't try to feel like you have to validate your experiences through your writing to make them relatable to others.

I'm afraid I don't trust my self to express, do, or execute – in my work and my life. Now feeling safe enough to dream, to take my time with my dreams, but not too much that I never execute – because I want to make room for new dreams. I can appreciate the process of continuing to sharpen my ability to actualize a vision, center meaningful progress, and explore what joy and happiness feel like in the midst of all of that.

The expression changes over time, but you are the essence that informs the expression. So you have to invest and hold space for your self, and put in your 10,000 hours to continuously evolve your craft and the expressions that come from it.

My perspective now is that instead of waiting for the working world to shift for me, I must resist it or avoid the work of moving slowly through life by prioritizing work in every moment.

I'm learning to let the writing be enough. I don't want to feel like I have to bring stories to life in very convoluted ways, or that my writing is only valid if I assert my opinion in a very intellectually or morally arrogant way. The writing – and I – are enough.

To Be Levelly Human

> "We reject pedestals, queenhood, and walking ten paces behind. To be recognized as human, levelly human, is enough." – Combahee River Collective Statement (1977)[42]

I am done being hard on my self with the assumption that certain outcomes are all within my control – what she needed was understanding, compassion, empathy, and for someone to help guide her through processing life and its inherent abstractness.

The most fully realized version of my self as I imagine her may not ever exist – and she still deserves a chance and I still deserve grace as I make my way towards her. My vision is worth the investment – in both the finances and other resources, as well as from the people and community around me and my work.

It's not about the logistics of my goals, dreams, and ambition – it's about sitting with and confronting my feelings about and relationship with my self and my ambition, my hopes, and dreams. It's not about being realistic about my dreams, but about grounding those dreams in reality. Instead of building worlds as an escape – I now see it as a bridge to the life I dream for my self.

Because the reality is – being a successful Black woman with a large platform just for the sake of having a large platform makes you vulnerable…exposed. I'd easily forgo that for a quiet and peaceful life where I can build a solid enough community around my work for the impact to be meaningful and tangible, and a big enough bank account to properly take care of my self and fund my project ideas.

As you work to bring your creative visions to life, as you work to build your life, there are things that you learn and gain from the journey and things that are lost from it. Things you have to grieve even though the final product is beautiful and exactly what it needed to be.

You can't separate my humanity, my humanness from the words that I write in the pieces of writing that I produce. *I* can no longer separate my humanity, my humanness from the words that I write in the pieces of writing that I produce.

I often want to return to a time when I did more daydreaming about life without the immediate need to act on it. A time when I could just get lost in and enjoy the dream.

But when your dreams and idea of your positive potential cover up the fact that you don't truly know, love, and appreciate who and where you are at this present moment;

those dreams become a cage. You put your self on a trajectory of being remembered but never known.

I know and understand now, that I am not above the Earth. My ability to have more understanding, compassion, and empathy for my self – allows me to have that for others.

So when I thought about that disconnect, or when I felt it when it came to sharing who I was becoming in my public life with friends and family it's always uncomfortable. Because maybe there is this chasm in who I show up as in more private and intimate spaces is not as confident or comfortable with being fully seen.

There is a smallness and powerlessness in acknowledging and accepting the responsibility that you have for your own life and journey. There's freedom in being honest and realistic.

Instead of allowing your self to hide behind aspiration and the work of being ambitious, sit with the discomfort of working towards self-knowledge and acceptance.

What do those dreams, visions, and ideas allow you to bring to the present moment? Curiosity? A willingness to sit through uncomfortable moments of non-resolution and transition to arrive on the other side and listen to the next set of questions you're being invited to explore?

On the other side of this – I know I want to be a woman who honors the truth of what she wants, who also has a deep respect for the Universe. Who trusts her self to show up and execute, but who also embodies what it means to be still and trusts that what she's said she desires is making its way to her.

I don't need to know exactly how the story ends, I just want to know that it is at least possible. I need tangible proof that transformation is not only possible, but that it can come to me with ease.

I want the freedom and agency to see and feel and experience life for my self; to choose and decide for my self; to build a life and experiences within it from that place of agency and clarity.

I want to be clear and honest and decisive with my self first about what I want so that I can more effectively discern what is for me or not, with what alliance with my desires or not. Or, at the very least, if there's something that moves me enough to want to learn more if I'm not immediately clear.

I want to feel safe and free to be more expressive about who I am and what I do and what I think and feel.

I want to view things from a beginner's mind – in both living and writing.

I want the regular, but I also want the remarkable. Equal parts ordinary and life-changing. Roots and wings. I want everything that is meant to be mine and everything that I can begin to imagine for my self.

I want to live in a way that is personally liberating while working towards liberation for my communities.

I want to be hopeful about the big things again. And I want to be happy in real life.

I feel the burden of life weighing so heavily on me at times – when I feel like I should be young and free of that pressure. But maybe this is also the time to explore and learn and be intentional about the foundational choices I make about my life's journey.

I want to prioritize being rooted in community, and I want to see the whole sky – to have the freedom and agency and autonomy to get to know the world for my self.

That requires me to know how to be both grounded, and in tune with my self to know when I feel called to move, which has been transformational for my relationship with my self. Even though other people or the world may view Black women as capable of doing everything under the Sun, that doesn't mean I have to accept the invitation blindly knowing that it isn't sustainable, nor is it the real work.

That work doesn't feel as urgent anymore – it's just how I've organized my life. I'm curious as to how I can better integrate and act on what I learned to see what outcomes I can create from what I learned and the opportunities I had to act on what I learned. Then I can make space for new knowledge.

I feel like I finally have space to enjoy the life that I am building for my self, and the fruits that are beginning to show from that labor. Being a vessel for my younger self's dreams requires that I treat my self in the present as worthy of investing in, pouring into, and maintaining.

I want to learn to respect my self enough to honor the pacing and journey of my life. Not pursuing my dreams – in whatever form they manifest at a particular season in my life – previously felt like a form of disrespect to my self. But, at this point, I've done enough to know that I'm capable of trying.

Because I only ever remembered seeing women close to me managing families and their daytime careers, but without seeing how full their lives were outside of that, I internalized the directive to pursue success. However, I didn't think to include healthy relationships or self-care as an imperative part of experiencing balance and sustainability in that pursuit. We think that focusing on relationships is a separate indulgence, rather than a fundamental aspect of our wellness and quality of life.

Our gifts and talents should be used for something more meaningful, our time and energy should be spent on living; connecting…loving.

You're not as compartmentalized as society wants to make us feel. Black women are made to be these tough, perpetually-resilient hustlers, and then we've adopted that mentality to transform it into something positive. It's not inherently bad, but when that identity is dependent on the denial of our self-care, our relational care, then it becomes a problem.

Upon deeper reflection, I now know that I also saw the Black women in my life with their friends, being loved out loud. I picked up on the success and career, not the relationships that can support you through that. I see my friends who are passionate about and successful at what they do in life, who are finding their way to that success, and who are also living life. Both are possible.

How are we continuing to deepen that process of holding our selves with compassion and care as we strive toward success? How are we making space to prioritize our relationships and not just romantic relationships? Again, romantic relationships aren't inherently a bad thing, but we are taught in society that – especially in cishet relationships – that being a successful partner as a Black woman requires you to twist and mold and change your self until you are no longer recognizable. I don't care to participate in that. Nor do I want to participate in a working world that also requires you to twist and mold and change your self for arbitrary metrics of success.

There is of course something to be said about women's roles in society, particularly for Black women, and how the home has historically been a site of oppression for us at the hands of both white folks and Black men. Yet and still, the real work of life is not necessarily out there, it is in our homes, our spirits, our practices of care for our selves and one another.

What does it mean to live in your life? To stop being afraid of embodying your own story, embracing it as yours – and that not being a bad thing. Meaning, going from only viewing your self as an extension of your familial or cultural legacy or social groups or peers.

Therapy Homework – July 29, 2020

Write a narrative about who I am as a person. What qualities do I already possess inside me, how do I feel about that, what things do I like about my self, what do I enjoy, what brings me peace?

One quality I love about my self is my ability to dream. That's what helps me be a better writer, to be able to imagine a world completely different from what I see in front of me. A better world, more than what is currently available to me. A subsequent quality I have since developed is the ability to work to actualize my dreams and visions. I recognized that it isn't enough to keep your dreams locked inside and that it is worth the effort to give your self the best possible shot at making them real. The journey since that realization has led me to more growth – growth that challenges who I am and to not settle or get comfortable with whatever I'm offered first in life.

Additionally, I love my optimism. I love when I'm able to rest, have fun and be free. I try to find pockets of that wherever I go. I enjoy learning, traveling, and following bursts of curiosity. I love expanding my perception of what exists and what is possible in the world. I would say reading allows me to do that from the comfort of my home, or anywhere really, which brings me peace – that I can satisfy that curiosity about the world and about other peoples' experiences and imaginations without really having to leave my place of comfort.

All of my goals are future-oriented but I feel like I wrote that because when I was younger it sounded good. It sounded good to be super invested in my future and have all the plans. Now, I want to be more present, be more intentional about integrating what I have learned into my actual daily living (how am I being the person I hope to become in this moment. Moment to moment, am I reaching towards my highest self or am I falling back to old habits and ways of being?). Cultivating the life I want to live requires integrating the person I believe my self to be in my inner world, and using her as an actor in my material experience, not just reserving her for my self and my imagination.

I am more than my career aspirations. I'm proud of my self for what I've been able to do for my self, the investments I've been courageous enough to make in my self to be my best and have the best. There is still more work to be done, and more fear to be overcome, but I've made significant progress in my relationship with my self and my life. I enjoy being a co-creator with God and the Universe.

What does it mean to build a full life? I'm no longer looking at the singular avenue of career and work as the only site of self-actualization.

My definition of success now is that I want to put in more energy and intention behind living my life, and building my self up as a person over the long term. Rather than pursuing and building up another thing – a career, a significant other, etc., and leaving my self as the last thing on my to-take-care-of list. Even still, there's a way of approaching this that could either perpetuate the paradigm of self-denial or usher in a new approach that asks, "What does it mean to live a life in service to your self?" before asking "What does it mean to live a life in service to others."

And that doesn't mean I can't do both – the point is that focusing on external directives for what success looks like as a young Black woman, is fickle and will change with the times. I want to be a part of the movements to foster new paradigms of what it means to live successfully and to have all that one desires. Where I don't have to compromise the "what," because I know my community will have my back on the "how."

I still want to be a leader and actualize my vision, but with a renewed sense of clarity around how. I want enough to be comfortable and to have something to pass on to my kids, where money isn't a stressor that I'm constantly worried about because my and my folks' needs are taken care of. I want to lead and empower and inspire young Black women and people to be their best selves – holistically. I want my skills and my knowledge, my time and energy, and other resources to go into my community, and my loved ones, rather than some arbitrary corporation or organization whose bottom line does not impact (or actively harms) my community.

If the past few years of living and writing this book have illustrated to me, unequivocally – is that I cannot move into the next chapter of my life without my community and a village.

I used to think success and fulfillment meant creating a checklist of tasks and rigid definitions of roles I would one day start requiring from people in my life, but really it has meant accepting, owning, and being radically honest about my human fallibility – the simple fact that I need, and I've always needed, people.

My perspective of excellence when it comes to work and what I do for a living looks like less work and more impact, now.

I very badly just want to have a good life – whatever that ends up looking like. Maybe that's as simple as a mindset shift, or it's as deep as needing to upend everything that I've come to know about my self and my world to find good in something, someone, or somewhere else.

Instead of trying to be everything and everywhere to see what sticks, it may feel better to spend time regrounding and reconnecting, and building a life from there – from a more integrated and embodied place.

Then, build exceptionality through a practice of deep self-knowledge, moving in alignment and integrity with your values, and holding steadfast to your belief in your own and the world's positive potential.

But first, you have to care about your self and your life. And I care about my self more than I care about my dreams for the sake of having them, or for the idea of achieving them. Fight for the space to honor your humanity.

I so often have wanted to fast forward to being the version of my self that has the knowledge and wisdom. But I know now that this way of thinking defeats the purpose of the journey, the reward is the hard-won knowledge and wisdom gained from being present for every step of the journey, the uncertainty and the discomfort, the trial and error, the learning and the realizations. I now fully see and am open to what it means to make my desires known, to do my part to orient my heart and mind toward them, and to make space in my life to receive them.

There's a quote – "her heart wants roots but her mind wants wings." My question lately has become – how do I make space for both?

I think a lot about the possibility that lies in this next phase of my life – continuing to learn and grow and be a student of life. I've always wanted children, to start and grow a family – and revisiting that has taught me that while I've dreamt about public and professional success, I've truly only ever wanted to be well-rounded, to simply live, and just be happy with my people.

Of course, due to the society that we live in, I still feel the external drive and necessity to play the game of material success and accomplishments that a life well-lived. But I am rooted in knowing that I very much want both.

I want both – the roots and wings. I feel more and more conflicted about that. I'm less attracted to the internalization of that I have to choose between or settle for either. I realize more and more that I'm less willing to internalize the world's shortcomings and limitations as my own. That is not – rather, that is no longer – mine to carry. What is mine to carry is the ongoing work of better understanding my self – of remaining aligned with my inner truth – so I can better advocate for those wants and needs. So I can have less shame in seeking support, and before that, in simply making those needs known to my self and others.

I'm open to a different calling that God has on my life.

I am open to the potential and possibility, not because I can't see it or don't believe it, but because I think that believing that acting like I believe it has caused me to forfeit my human needs for support, care, and being seen beyond what I'm capable of providing. I am open to the idea of spending the rest of my days simply learning and growing and running my race. Because to be human, levelly human, is enough.

Journal – November 1, 2020

I am cultivating a life where the default is connection and community (healthy, consenting, empowering, caring, loving) and I have the agency and respect from those I'm in community with to isolate when needed to recharge and recenter.

I know how to create a sturdy center for my self.

<u>*What I want to focus on in this season of my life:*</u>

- *Black feminist framework – recentering my work on that foundation*
- *Uplifting young Black writers*
- *Empowering young Black folks from across disciplines and walks of life to find their voices and use them in support of Black liberation.*
- *Personal empowerment and self-actualization, community empowerment and community engagement*

<u>*I'm not interested in:*</u>

- *Making everything about me (i.e. careerism), but still honoring and valuing my self and the vision God gave me to bring into the world*
- *Basing my work pace on election cycles, terms [of office], or other false measures of time*
- *Overstating my role and level of responsibility – refocus work on my communities and spaces*

* * *

What does healing look and feel like for me?

Maybe it's practicing patience, grace, and compassion with my self and others "even and especially in moments when we make mistakes." Setting and managing expectations upfront with clear systems of support and not moving forward if I don't have that.

Not internalizing or personalizing moments when I've made mistakes, let my ego/insecurities/past hurts get the best of me. By talking about it and moving through it – not around it by avoiding it – and feeling it, I am growing and evolving rather than continuing to push shit down and avoid my self.

The things that bring me hope, excitement, and happiness include exploring my curiosity, freedom, personal potential, and agency. Opening my self up to more ease, love, connection, and peace. Before that felt simple (like bad simple) and frivolous and self-indulgent.

Yet the things I *should* want – material success and career achievements, status among my peers in my community, responsibility, and value to others – feel too big and abstract. One is a distraction, a barrier, to the other.

Spend too much time on one end and you're too serious and stuck up. On the other end, you're not taking your life and its responsibilities seriously enough, your head's in the clouds.

Don't Call Me a Content Creator (part two)

As I've thought about what it might be like to have a more traditional career in media, I still feel like I've spent a lot of time and energy over the past few years on projects and goals that served others' visions, or that hindered my vision by being consumed with how I thought other people would perceive it and whether or not it, and I would be taken seriously.

301

On top of that, leaving school for the first time in 2019 and then learning I have ADHD before I left for the second time in 2021 further unraveled the attachment of my worth and value to worldly success. Which led to the unraveling of major parts of my identity – who I believed my self to be, for better and worse, and what my priorities were.

Through all of those moments – which on deeper reflection pointed to a lifetime of experiences – I recognized that I internalized a really powerful and pervasive inner critic out of fear of facing the possibility that maybe those people were right: that my authentic self and my contributions are actually not good or worthy or needed.

Before college, I started a blog to create a space to have more control and intention with how I shared my voice and, really, my self. It was a way for me to document (albeit publicly) my process of self-discovery by expressing my thoughts and feelings about a variety of topics.

Through journalism, I was able to extend that approach by covering topics that I found interesting or that resonated with me, bringing awareness to things happening in Black communities, and learning from community leaders working to address them in the process.

These roles of being someone who cared deeply about my agency and individuality when it came to my voice, coupled with my aspirations of being taken seriously as a writer and media professional – lead to the idea of having to center my self publicly to bring attention to my work feeling icky and unnecessary, but I also recognize that the things I wrote about and shared matter because I wrote them, just as much as what I wrote in and of itself.

I remembered how powerful a tool that writing is for me to simply gather and explore my thoughts, feelings, and ideas. When I decided in 2019 to write a book's worth of essays, the writing process was for me to work through present and past emotions and experiences. I spent a lot of time unsure if I would actually finish it, or if I would publish it if I did.

My fears about writing again and putting out this book ring true to my fears about showing up fully and authentically as a human being: *How deeply are people actually willing to engage me and my work? What if people don't think it's good? What if it's not objectively good?*

Especially today, with the lines between "content creators" and writers and journalists and communicators being blurred significantly.

Not that you have to share things about your personal and private life to build a brand, but the requisites for grasping people's attention on the internet today feel exemplified by oversharers on TikTok, podcast bros; lifestyle, couple and family vloggers on YouTube whose stories inevitably end in joint breakup video statements and shitty apology videos; and general anxiety about whether your close friends content is interesting enough to warrant people's attention.

While this has allowed more people to have access to the

tools and knowledge to make creative content, it also hasn't necessarily come with editorial standards including things like fact-checking that also fuel misinformation and enable shitty media literacy and consumption practices. Much of it is what will grab people's attention fast, even if it's flagrant and inflammatory, or just blatantly not correct and people think they're amplifying accurate information.

I also think this world and society, by and large, do not teach us the importance of – or even how to – explore and discover our selves, and see that as a separate endeavor from doing what you need to do to survive or meet a basic human need for attention and love and belonging or achieve material success.

I'm very much still exploring what it means to be human and be a writer, let alone what I want a career as a writer to look like. I know that lives and careers – both practices – take time to build.

What I want is to not feel afraid to take up space within my self, my life, my relationships – and to allow that to anchor me as I explore how I want to take up space elsewhere in the world.

I've done a lot of work to enjoy the journey of living for living's sake, rather than living solely to get interesting content. I still want to document my life and my journey, but it doesn't feel as *necessary* as it did before. Now it just feels like work – and there are parts of that that scare me, and other parts that remind me of the dreamer I knew my self to be two or even four years ago.

I know that at that time, I wanted (and needed) to seek clarity, explore my ideas and curiosities, and potential, at a pace and in a way that I could decide and have control and agency over. But I also subconsciously was overcompensating for and hoping to one day receive validation that I was on the right path, and ultimately I think for that deeper connection and belonging. Whole time, that was never God's intention for me and I did my self a disservice by cutting off my mouthpiece for me to connect directly with my readers, human to human, and not founder or employee or board member to market. If I waited for the validation and approval of other writers, publications or publishers, readers, and even my loved ones, I would have done nothing and gotten nowhere.

I've been thinking a lot about what it means to get back into writing for my self creatively again, but also about what it would mean to build an archive of my work. I dream about building and facilitating community spaces online and offline not only for the production of content and storytelling, but to talk about and engage more deeply with the work and ideas shared in said content.

For me, social media is (and I believe, should be) about the promotion and distribution of my work and a means to connect with my audience, rather than the sum total of my work itself. At this point, I don't mind just sharing that work in the void and hoping other people find it valuable and important. I just want to create and share. I guess going viral isn't the point, but I also would love for my work to reach and have a positive impact on as many people as possible.

It feels incredibly fickle to aspire to work endlessly to contribute my limited human time and energy to create things that dissipate into the digital atmosphere: I did that with pieces from the blog I started in high school, along with bylines from my earliest internships, however, most of them just disappeared with website re-builds or with people just deciding the pieces were no longer relevant. There are memories associated with those pieces, along with burnout that has had real-life implications on my health (more than it should for my age) and time spent that I'm not going to get back – even though I may be "young with a whole career ahead of me."

So much of my early 20s and early career experience has left me feeling like I was seen and positioned as a machine that is expected to constantly produce content. There was little to no room to sit with and explore ideas, think critically about what you wanted to say and why, research, or focus on the selection and use of each word and phrase to find the perfect one. Just the final product of content.

I have never had the desire to and now I can't constantly cater to manufactured "short attention spans" and people simply not wanting to read and engage thoughtfully with ideas. I absolutely am committed to finding creative and innovative ways to make my written work more accessible and baking that into my process. But I am done uncritically bending to ever-changing social media and digital algorithms and expectations that cater to the attention economy and a culture that enables shitty media and information consumption practices.

Sources of satisfaction for me in my writing include discovering and claiming my autonomy, agency, and ownership of my work and contributions. I find it in exploring deeper levels of my identity and lived experience, in using my writing as a way to connect with people authentically through the creation process and the final piece. I love exploring how to connect my own personal experiences and pop culture moments to larger social issues or universal experiences in the human condition.

I want to have more positive experiences and memories associated with getting to explore ideas, dig into writing, express my self, and connect with other people who like nerding out on their crafts and ideas, processes, etc.

And I want to create a body of work that represents my interests and curiosities, that punctuates my growth as a human being and woman, that illustrates how certain things change and evolve but the essence of you stays the same throughout all of that.

I used to feel like I didn't have the time and space to write about topics and issues that I care most deeply about – specifically pieces that find a balance of creative writing and cultural commentary on sociopolitical issues, rather than hyperfocus on social justice issues in a way that feels boring and like posturing, rather than finding new angles in that resonate more deeply with people. But I realized, especially after beginning the journey to write these essays, that I was giving my self space and time to think about and come to – not necessarily conclusions, but my truth or clarity in my own perception – about those issues as it relates to the vantage point of my lived experience.

I believe I have done a good job at beginning to work to rebuild a healthy self-concept beyond my aspirations, and beyond what the world says about young neurodivergent Black girls from the South, the journey to which is documented in the essays of this book.

Now that I'm essentially at the finish line, I also feel like I have limited my self in some ways out of fear of being that same naive dreamer that I was, so this book is also a transition point for me to get back to the work that I most deeply enjoy – the work of being human, and exploring that work through my creative writing.

I have appreciated the time and space over the past 3 1/2 years or so to think about who I am and am becoming, as I write and work on this project. I believe I am now transitioning into a time of more sharing, and I'm ready to make space for newer ideas, feelings, and experiences.

Before that, though, I don't know that I gave my self credit for how I carried my self through that time of deep uncertainty – moving from a period of basing my contentment and value off of external achievements (or the perceived potential of those outcomes).

I continued to show up for my self – for my past self that wasn't sure what would be on the other side of that situation, as well as my future self, who is so much wiser and more at peace because of the choices I made to get here.

There was a time when I truly did not see anything past 25 – for no other reason than because I was playing a very short-sighted game that required me to decenter my self and my needs.

All of this is still part of my story, but I am putting that down, for good, and opening my self up to the potential of experiencing my self and my life more deeply and embodied than what I've previously allowed my self.

A New Dawn

For continuity, let's revisit the original question posed at the beginning of this book regarding the Hero's Journey:

> *"But the question remains: What is there to be gained by risking the plunge into one's depths? What do heroes find in the underworld or at bottoms of oceans? Eliade responds, 'One goes down into the belly of a giant or monster in order to learn science or wisdom.' The hero is now a person who knows. He has learned the mysteries surrounding life and is one who was given revelations that are metaphysical in nature. To face one's demons and to succeed in taming them implies that one no longer fears the disintegration of the self. Such initiation is tantamount to transcending death anxiety. And this wish is exactly at the core of all heroes' innermost desires."*

(222)

If we keep reading, the part after gets at something interesting:

"Heroes long for more than inner cohesion. Since the Self is directly linked to and influenced by the unconscious, and since the latter, for Jung, has collective dimensions, it ensures that the self sought after by heroes is not just an 'Inner Self' but also a 'World Self.' Jung defined such a Self as an ideal image we all long for. It is the image of the divine, of God within us. The Self heroes seek is therefore tantamount to aspiring to be godlike. It thus follows that one's true Self is found in being actively involved in communal life and in the daily attempts to improve the human condition through love, respect, and reverence." (222)

What I was working towards was internal clarity – now what kind of life can I build with that foundation?

I now feel moved to work towards more congruence to find alignment between the person I am and who I am working toward becoming. In addition to working on this book, I've gone to therapy and done a lot of self-reflection. The most important tool in my toolbox, though, has undoubtedly been learning to be present in my process – to sit in the uncomfortable emotions and remain steadfast in my commitment to not avoid the work or my self.

Getting comfortable with the discomfort that comes with

genuine growth, as does attending to my emotional regulation, and not putting my self in situations where I just expect perfection and excellence without actually doing the work.

Where I would previously isolate my self and prevent my self from experiencing deeper forms of connection and vulnerability; I have learned to instead reduce the noise and find space and time to focus on what I need (it's different, trust me).

I'm able to more easily extend my self grace –unlearning the internalized expectation to have it all figured out. It's helped me feel more at ease in my life.

From this point, I hope to continue building a deeply authentic life. One in which the choices I make and the rules I play by are all aligned with a clear view of my needs, wants, and desires for my self in this life.

I'm also hopeful that with this blank page, I can write the next chapter in the story of my relationship with my self. From here, I can start from a more confident place to explore how good it can get. To explore how to co-create with God and the Universe to build a life that is more honest and aligned.

Truthfully, I'm just happy to be here. To have the awareness to lean into each moment as an endless journey of learning and deepening my relationship with my self, God, the Universe, and my community. To have the opportunity to learn how to balance faith with curiosity about who you are and who you are becoming.

I trust God to lead me to where I'm going, I trust the Universe to make space for me, and I trust my self to honor the choices that I meant to make to get us there.

There were times I would keep trying to start each "new beginning" with the same perspective, tools, and approach... What would it mean to truly give my self permission to start again?

In writing, at least, lies an opportunity to give my past self the gift of someone coming along aspects of my journey with me. Even if I didn't have that in real-time, there is something comforting about knowing that version of my self – her thoughts, feelings, and experiences – will have the chance to be seen and heard, on her terms.

In living, I'd also like to think that I'm offering my future self an opportunity to experience ease, joy, lightness...happiness.

I used to think that happiness was an arbitrary goal, that meaning was a more important focus of my time and energy. But now that I feel like I have worked to experience a sense of meaning in my life, I now understand that I just want to be happy in the simplest of ways.

The balance between creating and holding and maintaining the space for me to get deep into my emotional self to write in a voice that is authentic and clear; and doing the same for my self to be light and free to live a life that is also authentic and clear.

Journal – February 6, 2019

If my life had absolutely no limits, what would I choose to have and what would I choose to do?

I would choose a life where I can accomplish all of my professional goals and purpose while remaining healthy, whole, fulfilled, and connected to the people I love and care most about. That's definitely possible with limits, but I feel like the capitalist society in which we live promotes an unhealthy and unfulfilling lifestyle where hard work and achievements come before people, and that is not a life I want to lead. I would start a business where I can create meaningful content and tell the stories of underrepresented individuals and communities, do meaningful work that goes beyond content but results in real-life, positive change for the various issues that plague our world. I would travel often with my family and friends to countries with rich cultures, good food, beaches, beautiful scenes, and familial roots (Spain, Greece, Cameroon, Ghana, Cuba, etc.). I would be a plant lady, a wife, and the mother of three children. I would help my friends reach their individual purpose, either with services or support. I would have nationwide or even global influence without being disconnected from the communities that have fostered my growth and that of my family.

* * *

Whatever happens from this point forward, I know that God still wants me to be happy – to experience deep joy – despite my depression and disappointment.

Maybe there is still an opportunity to build a beautiful life.

And maybe the point was for me to realize that was the case all along.

Our lives can often look like an incline to others on the outside but only you and I know how it's begun and ended and begun more times than I can count.

My Dad once said, "Life is hard, find your joy." And I think for young people – the lowercase 't' trauma of not being clear on who and how you want to be in the world can be that hard thing that keeps us from experiencing self-acceptance, peace, and joy in the present moment.

I'm finally at a point where I get joy from simply being alive. From getting to wake up and get another opportunity to continue living, learning, and laughing (#LiveLaughLove).

I can begin to imagine the next horizon – what it might be, what it might look and feel like.

So thank you, Dear Reader, for riding this journey, this part of my journey, with me. Here's to remembering to wedge some space between now and then, between the being and becoming. Here's to remembering that for now, there is lightness and the freedom to begin again.

Afterword

Epilogue: The Morning Always Comes

"There is something beautiful coming even if it's only the Sun" – Ashe Vernon

"What's past is prologue." – Shakespeare, The Tempest (1611)

Journal – June 13, 2020

What I thought would be a reflection on the past year of my life – the highs, lows, and lessons learned – is honestly a revelation that my spirit is moving me to look forward and be present. I now have a newfound motivation to act more consistently from a place of unwavering faith and radical hope.

For the first time in a long time, or at least for today, I'm releasing worry about the future and allowing my self to lean into joy in this present moment. And not out of avoidance – because if there's anything I've learned, Black joy has always existed in spite of struggle.

Doubly, if there's anything I've learned from being a Gemini, it's duality. That you can accept two, seemingly opposing truths at once. And even if you don't accept them, that doesn't negate their truth.

I feel aligned with a certain hunger and commitment to figuring my journey out as I go and not just allowing but leaning into moments of not knowing. I am learning to be okay with not knowing because it has left me with no other option than to be present. That is where I've found my personal power.

When I let go of the rigid idea of what I think life is supposed to be like, and how I think I am supposed to show up in it, I find much more wiggle room to truly explore and co-create something sacred with God.

When I search past my ego – the version of my self that clings to a false sense of control over her life – I find a deeply rooted gratitude for the opportunity to learn, grow, create, love, contribute, and evolve.

I believe I found that feeling in fleeting moments in the past. Almost as if God was showing me glimpses, just enough to remind me that there can be more to this life than I've always known to be true or allowed my self to settle for.

Imagination is defined as "the power of forming a mental image of something not present to the senses or never before wholly perceived in reality." This moment has inspired me to tap into my imagination, reminiscent of my inner child. A version of my self who does not just dream of but believes in a life and world where all good things are fully possible.

Today and every day moving forward, I promise my self to keep my face towards the rising Sun[43]. To be intentional about not only looking forward to it but actively preparing for it. Actively embodying it. Because "weeping may tarry for the night, but joy comes in the morning." And the morning always comes.

About the Cover

After visiting the Smithsonian's National Museum of African Art for visual inspiration, I viewed this oil painting – titled 'Sunshine Land' by Tchif, an artist from Benin, in an exhibition titled *Earth Matters: Land as Material and Metaphor in the Arts of Africa.*[44]

Sunshine Land, *by Tchif (2012)*

The red line in the painting, which the Museum describes as possibly representing "the journey of a soul through life on Earth," inspired the yellow line which moves through the cover of the book.

The symbol in the middle of the book cover is the Adinkra symbol "Owia Kokroko" – which means "Greatness of the Sun" in Twi, a dialect of the Akan language spoken in Ghana, and can symbolize vitality, enlightenment, and renewal.

The 'Owia Kokroko' symbol

Notes

PREFACE

1 An Identity Crisis Is Vital For Growth Because It Occurs At The Edge Of Chaos And Harmony – by Tony Fahkry | Mission.org (Medium – https://medium.com/the-mission/an-identity-crisis-is-vital-for-growth-because-it-occurs-at-the-edge-of-chaos-and-harmony-78c713d49879)

LAND ACKNOWLEDGMENTS

2 Kimmerer, Robin Wall. 2015. *Braiding Sweetgrass*. Minneapolis, MN: Milkweed Editions.

THE REALIZATION OF A NEGRO'S AMBITION

3 The Realization of a Negro's Ambition (1916) [Lost Film] – Department of Afro American Research Arts & Culture (https://www.daaracarchive.org/2016/10/the-realization-of-negros-ambition-1916.html)

4 Materiality: "[T]he exploration of the situated experiences of material life, the constitution of the object world and concomitantly its shaping of human experience." – Stanford University Department of Anthropology (https://anthropology.stanford.edu/research-projects/materiality)

5 "Sex X Money X Sneakers" – by BJ The Chicago Kid, *P I N E A P P L E N O W- L A T E R S* (2012)

6 How Black Middle-Class Kids Become Poor Adults – by Gillian B. White | *The Atlantic* (https://www.theatlantic.com/business/archive/2015/01/how-black-middle-class-kids-become-black-lower-class-adults/384613/)

7 Maslow's Hierarchy of Needs (https://www.simplypsychology.org/maslow.html)

ME? A HERO?

321

8   Coelho, Paulo. 1995. *The Alchemist*. London, England: Thorsons.

9   "Cinderella" – by The Cheetah Girls, The Cheetah Girls (Movie Soundtrack – 2003)

10   Hero's Journey Theory of Joseph Campbell: Analytical Overview – EduBirdie (https://edubirdie.com/examples/heros-journey-theory-of-joseph-campbell-analytical-overview/)

11   Lacocque, Pierre-E. "Fear of Engulfment and the Problem of Identity." *Journal of Religion and Health* 23, no. 3 (1984): 218–28. http://www.jstor.org/stable/27505784.

WHEN GOD SPEAKS THROUGH YOUR UBER DRIVER

12   The Case for Reparations – by Ta-Nehisi Coates | *The Atlantic* (https://www.theatlantic.com/magazine/archive/2014/06/the-case-for-reparations/361631/)

TO LIVE IN THE WORLD AND NOT IN MY HEAD

13   "Circus" – by Britney Spears, *Circus* (2008)

14   "Yellow" – by Aminé, Good for You (2017)

15   Reference: Intuition (Lemonade Poem, Part 1) – written by Warsan Shire, performed by Beyoncé (https://genius.com/Beyonce-intuition-lemonade-poem-part-1-annotated)

16   Interview with André 3000 – Broken Record, Hosted by Rick Rubin (https://www.youtube.com/watch?v=LjHcHTJ8D5k)

17   Marshall, Hermine. (1989). The Development of Self-Concept. Young Children (https://www.researchgate.net/publication/234644683_The_Development_of_Self-Concept)

18   Osho. *Love, Freedom, and Aloneness* (2003)

19   Kevin Quashie, *The Sovereignty of Quiet: Beyond Resistance in Black Culture* (2012)

20   Ellison, Thomas. Slavery and Secession in America: Historical and Economical. United Kingdom: S. Low, Son & Company, 1862.

ON BEING YOUNG, A WOMAN, AND COLORED

21   On Being Young — a Woman — and Colored – by Marita O. Bonner (https://www.literaryladiesguide.com/full-texts-of-classic-works/on-being-young-a-woman-and-colored-marita-o-bonner-1925/)

22   Audre Lorde, *Learning from the 60s – Speech* (https://www.blackpast.or
g/african-american-history/1982-audre-lorde-learning-60s/)

23   **References**:
Understanding Personal Agency (https://philosophicaltherapist.co
m/2017/03/21/understanding-personal-agency/)
Subjugation as a Tool for Agency (https://erinschaefer.net/subjugat
ion-as-a-tool-for-agency/)

24   Why we mourn girlhood – by Katy Waldman | *The New Yorker* (https://w
ww.newyorker.com/books/under-review/why-we-mourn-girlhood)

25   The patriarchy expects you to follow these scripts – by Pumla Dineo
Gqola | *New Frame* (https://www.newframe.com/the-patriarchy-expe
cts-you-to-follow-these-scripts/)

26   Freire on Freedom of Education – Knowledge, Education, and Identity
(https://scholarblogs.emory.edu/basicproblems002/2015/03/30/frei
re-on-freedom-of-education/)

27   Projection and Inner Reality – FrithLuton.com (https://frithluton.com/
articles/projection-inner-reality/)

DON'T BE A LADY, BE A LEGEND

28   *'Daddy's Little Girls'* Actress Gabrielle Union – NPR News (https://www
.npr.org/2007/02/09/7304620/daddys-little-girls-actress-gabrielle-
union)

29   The Uses of Anger: Women Responding to Racism – by Audre Lorde
(1981 – https://www.blackpast.org/african-american-history/speec
hes-african-american-history/1981-audre-lorde-uses-anger-women-
responding-racism/)

30   Wikipedia contributors, "Optimal distinctiveness theory," *Wikipedia,
The Free Encyclopedia,* https://en.wikipedia.org/w/index.php?title=Op
timal_distinctiveness_theory&oldid=1146227913

31   The Trap of Thinking You're Special and Entitled to Success – by Mosab
Alkhteb | Tiny Buddha (https://tinybuddha.com/blog/trap-thinking-
youre-special-entitled-success/)

BECAUSE IT'S BETTER TO SPEAK...

32   Brené Brown on the necessity of facing and confronting your self –
TikTok by Kendall Coffman Therapy (@kcoffmantherapy – https://w
ww.tiktok.com/@kcoffmantherapy/video/7137489933085887790)

33 The Romanticization of Howard University – by Kési Felton (https://k
    esifelton.medium.com/the-romanticization-of-howard-university-8
    c161d0a3cd3)

34 Interview with Adrienne Manns-Israel (http://digital.wustl.edu/e/eii/
    eiiweb/man5427.0075.101adriennemanns-israel.html)

    Also see: Leaders of Howard University takeover reflect 50 years later
    Los Angeles Sentinel (https://lasentinel.net/leaders-of-howard-unive
    rsity-takeover-reflect-50-years-later.html)

35 Why the Problem with Learning Is Unlearning – by Mark Bonchek |
    Harvard Business Review (https://hbr.org/2016/11/why-the-proble
    m-with-learning-is-unlearning)

36 The Institutional Order: Economy, Kinship, Religion, Polity, Law, and
    Education in Evolutionary and Comparative Perspective – by Jonathan
    H. Turner (https://books.google.com/books/about/The_Institutional
    _Order.html?id=dY7ZAAAAMAAJ)

37 Value vs Mores – What's the difference? | WikiDiff (https://wikidiff.co
    m/value/mores)

38 Structure (definition) | Open Education Sociology Dictionary (https://s
    ociologydictionary.org/structure/)

39 For bell hooks (1952-2021) – by Julius Gavroche | Autonomies (https://a
    utonomies.org/2021/12/for-bell-hooks-1952-2021/)

40 A Litany for Survival – by Audre Lorde | Poetry Foundation (https://w
    ww.poetryfoundation.org/poems/147275/a-litany-for-survival)

41 The Transformation of Silence into Language and Action* – by Audre
    Lorde (https://drive.google.com/file/d/1bIR1IIMQ_gERcAFEwoP_
    7GncTooKrdDK/view?usp=sharing)

STORYTELLER. DREAM WEAVER. WISE WOMAN.

42 The Combahee River Collective Statement (1977 – https://www.blac
    kpast.org/african-american-history/combahee-river-collective-state
    ment-1977/)

AFTERWORD

43 Reference: Lift Every Voice and Sing – by James Weldon Johnson (
    https://www.poetryfoundation.org/poems/46549/lift-every-voice-a
    nd-sing)

ABOUT THE COVER

44 *Earth Matters: Land as Material and Metaphor in the Arts of Africa,* The Smithsonian National Museum of African Art (https://africa.si.edu/exhibits/earthmatters/index.html)

About the Author

Kési Felton ('Casey' – she/her) is a writer from Acworth, Georgia. Through storytelling, her goal is to learn how to best leverage digital platforms to tell impactful stories that translate to lasting communities in real life.

She is also the founder and publisher of Better to Speak, a movement media platform for young and emerging Black storytellers.

You can connect with me on:
- https://www.kesifelton.com
- https://twitter.com/kesifelton
- https://www.facebook.com/kesifelton
- https://www.bettertospeak.org

Subscribe to my newsletter:

✉ https://kfandcompany.substack.com/?utm_source=substack&utm_medium=web&utm_campaign=reader2&utm_source=/search/kesi%20felton&utm_medium=reader2